Songs and Rhymes Readers Theatre for Beginning Readers

Anthony D. Fredericks

Readers Theatre

Teacher Ideas Press

An imprint of Libraries Unlimited
Westport, Connecticut • London

Library of Congress Cataloging-in-Publication Data

Fredericks, Anthony D.
  Songs and rhymes readers theatre for beginning readers / Anthony D. Fredericks.
  p. cm. — (Readers theatre)
  Includes bibliographical references and index.
  ISBN 978-1-59158-627-2 (alk. paper)
  1. Reading (Elementary)—United States. 2. Language arts (Primary)—United States. 3.
Literacy—United States. 4. Children's songs. 5. Nursery rhymes. I. Title.
  LB1573.L657 2008
  372.41—dc22   2007030921

British Library Cataloguing in Publication Data is available.

Library of Congress Catalog Card Number: 2007030921
ISBN: 978-1-59158-627-2

First published in 2008

Libraries Unlimited/Teacher Ideas Press, 88 Post Road West, Westport, CT 06881
A Member of the Greenwood Publishing Group, Inc.
www.lu.com

Printed in the United States of America

The paper used in this book complies with the
Permanent Paper Standard issued by the National
Information Standards Organization (Z39.48–1984).

10   9   8   7   6   5   4   3   2   1

Contents

Preface

Sing, sing, sing a song
With your student team.
Merrily, merrily, merrily, merrily,
Learning is a dream.

The rhymes and rhythms of language can be playfully shared with children by incorporating songs and other rhythmic events into your everyday activities. Songs are a playful way for children to learn about and utilize language in a variety of activities and sharing opportunities. They are wonderful ways to open up the school day, delightful introductions to lessons and specific learning activities, and creative ventures into using language across the curriculum.

A rhyming teacher came to town,
A-singing and a-dancing;
She stuck a feather in her hat,
And all the kids were prancing.

Rhyming teacher keep it up.
Rhyming teacher cherry,
Mind the music and the steps
And with the kids be merry.

Rhyming activities and projects are familiar components of most language arts programs for beginning readers. Often the rhyme patterns are silly—a feature that indicates to children the fun that can be had with words. Other times the rhyming patterns encourage listeners to create their own words or endings to lines—a further inducement to be active participants in the telling of a story. It's important to note that songs and rhymes have been proven to assist children in learning about how language functions in addition to the many ways in which language can be shared in a mutually supportive environment.

All around the mulberry bush,
The monkey chased the weasel.
The monkey thought 'twas all in fun.
Pop! Goes the weasel.

A penny for a spool of thread,
A penny for a needle.
That's the way the money goes.
Pop! Goes the weasel.

Certainly one of the most endearing qualities of songs and rhymes in the primary classroom is their overt humor. Animals stink, ants go marching in long drawn-out lines, old men bump their heads and can't get up in the morning, and a couple of folks spend their time doing a "skip to my Lou." The situations are ridiculous, exaggerated, and simply silly—just the kind of humor young kids love!

This book offers beginning readers a participatory approach to the wide and wonderful world of songs and rhymes. It is based on the idea that when students are provided with meaningful opportunities to make an "investment of self" in their education, that education will become both relevant and dynamic. *Songs and Rhymes Readers Theatre for Beginning Readers* presents readers theatre scripts that stimulate children to become active participants in popular and familiar literature. Students will sing songs, explore stories, play with words, and investigate cherished rhymes that are staples of their early literary experiences. In short, students will enact songs and rhymes that are engaging, delightful, and full of fun!

Within these pages is a dynamic variety of creative learning possibilities for your classroom or library. Here your students will discover an exciting potpourri of mind-expanding and concept-building experiences—experiences that will engage and excite them as beginning readers. Just as important: Your students will participate in positive learning experiences that can serve as a strong foundation for additional literary explorations in phonemic awareness, phonics, fluency, vocabulary, and comprehension development.

So, be prepared for lots of action, lots of drama, and lots of fun!

Ring around the classroom,
A pocket full of rhymin',
Laughing, singing
We all fall down!

Tony Fredericks

Introduction

Once upon a time I wrote two teacher resource books: *Nonfiction Readers Theatre for Beginning Readers* and *Mother Goose Readers Theatre for Beginning Readers* (both Teacher Ideas Press). These two books were specifically designed for teachers of grades 1–2 (all of the scripts were controlled for readability). Those books included scripts that celebrated the value of nonfiction literature as well as traditional Mother Goose adaptations—all specifically designed for students in the beginning stages of reading development.

Those books have found their way into thousands of primary-level classrooms and library programs around the country. Teachers use them as major elements of their overall language arts program. Librarians use them to introduce familiar (and unfamiliar) literature as part of their regular library offerings. Those books became popular and much-loved elements in children's initial introductions to literature and learning.

Comments I receive from educators across the country attest to the unbelievable joy that comes about when readers theatre is made part of classroom and library experiences. Typically, those messages celebrate three specific benefits of readers theatre:

1. **Fluency**—"I really like the way readers theatre provides my first grade students with positive models of language use that help build bridges between word recognition and comprehension."

2. **Integrated Language Arts**—"When children participate in readers theatre they can understand and appreciate the interrelationships between reading, writing, listening, and speaking . . . and literature!"

3. **Active Engagement**—"Readers theatre provides my students with many opportunities to become actively engaged in the dynamics of reading. They are participating, they are learning, and they are having loads of fun! What a joy!"

With the overwhelming success of those two books, it wasn't too long before teachers and librarians would approach me at conferences and in-service workshops asking for an additional volume of readers theatre scripts. They not only requested more scripts that could be used with beginning readers, but were equally interested in scripts that celebrated the rhythms and rhymes of language. Thus was born the idea for this book.

WHAT IS READERS THEATRE?

Readers theatre is a storytelling device that stimulates the imagination and promotes *all* of the language arts. Simply stated, it is an oral interpretation of a piece of literature read in a dramatic style. Readers theatre is an act of involvement, an opportunity to share, a time to creatively interact with others, and a personal interpretation of what can be or could be. Readers theatre provides numerous opportunities for youngsters to make stories and literature come alive and pulsate with their own unique brand of perception and vision. In so doing, literature becomes personal and reflective—children have a breadth of opportunities to be authentic users of language.

The magic of storytelling has been a tradition of every culture and civilization since the dawn of language. It binds human beings and celebrates their heritage as no other language art can. It is part and parcel of the human experience, because it underscores the values and experiences we cherish as well as those we seek to share with each other. Nowhere is this more important than in today's classroom or school library. Perhaps it is a natural part of who we are—that stories command our attention and help us appreciate the values, ideas, and traditions we hold dear. So, too, should students have those same experiences and those same pleasures.

Storytelling conjures up all sorts of visions and possibilities—faraway lands; magnificent themes; special characters; and certainly tales of mystery, intrigue, and adventure. These are stories that enchant, mystify, and excite through a marvelous weaving of characters, settings, and plots . . . tales that have stood the test of time. Our senses are stimulated, our mental images are energized, and our experiences are fortified through the magic of storytelling.

Storytelling is also a way of sharing the power and intrigue of language. I suppose part of my belief that storytelling is the quintessential classroom or library activity lies in the fact that it is an opportunity to bring life, vitality, and substance to the two-dimensional letters and words on a printed page. So too, is it an interpersonal activity—a "never-fail" way to connect with minds and souls and hearts.

When children are provided with regular opportunities to become storytellers, they develop a personal stake in the literature shared. They also begin to cultivate personal interpretations of that literature—interpretations that lead to higher levels of appreciation and comprehension. Practicing and performing stories is an involvement endeavor—one that demonstrates and utilizes numerous languaging activities. So too, do youngsters learn to listen to their classmates and appreciate a variety of presentations.

READERS THEATRE AND FLUENCY

Of no less importance is the significance of readers theatre as a method to enhance reading fluency. Reading researchers have identified five primary areas of reading instruction for all beginning readers. These include

❖ phonemic awareness,

❖ phonics,

❖ fluency,

❖ vocabulary, and

❖ comprehension.

When teachers and librarians incorporate readers theatre into their respective programs, youngsters are offered multiple opportunities to, as one first-grade teacher told me, "understand the natural rhythm and flow of language."

Fluency is the ability to read text accurately and quickly. It's reading in which words are recognized automatically. When fluent readers read, they group words quickly to help them gain meaning from what they read. Their oral reading sounds natural and their silent reading is smooth and unencumbered by an overemphasis on word-by-word analysis. Fluent readers are those who do not need to concentrate on the decoding of words; rather, they can direct their attention to comprehension of text. In short, fluent readers are able to recognize words and comprehend them at the same time. They are able to make connections between their background knowledge and ideas in a book or other piece of writing. I often like to think of fluency as the essential stepping stone between phonetic ability and comprehension.

It's important to remember that fluency is something that develops over time. Fluency instruction must be integrated into all aspects of the reading program as the "bridge" that students need to be successful comprehenders. Fluency is not an isolated element of the reading curriculum—rather, it is an essential component that models and provides active involvement opportunities for students as they transition from decoding to comprehension. A study by the National Assessment of Educational Progress (NAEP, 2001) found a direct correlation between fluency and reading comprehension. In fact, students who score low on measures of fluency also score low on measures of comprehension. The implication was that efforts designed to foster fluency development will have a direct impact on students' growth and development in comprehension development.

It is not surprising that one of the most effective ways teachers and librarians can promote fluency development—particularly for beginning readers—is through the use of readers theatre. Its advantages are twofold:

1. it offers positive models of fluent reading as demonstrated by a teacher or other accomplished readers, and

2. it provides beginning readers with a legitimate reason for rereading text in an enjoyable and engaging format.

Students get to practice fluency in authentic texts and in authentic situations. Reading is portrayed as a pleasurable activity—it has both purpose and interest. As students take on the roles of characters, they also take on the roles of competent readers.

WHAT IS THE VALUE OF READERS THEATRE?

I like to think of readers theatre as a way to interpret literature without the constraints of skills, rote memorization, or assignments. Readers theatre allows children to breathe life and substance into stories—an interpretation that is colored by kids' unique perspectives, experiences, and vision. It is, in fact, the readers' interpretation of an event that is intrinsically more valuable than some predetermined and/or preordained "translation" (something that might be found in a teacher's manual or curriculum guide, for example).

With that in mind, I'd like to share with you some of the many values I see in readers theatre:

❖ Readers theatre is a participatory event. The characters as well as the audience are all intimately involved in the design, structure, and delivery of the story. As such, children begin to realize that learning is not a solitary activity, but one that can be shared and discussed with others.

❖ It stimulates curiosity and enthusiasm for learning. It allows children to experience learning in a supportive and nonthreatening format that underscores their active involvement.

❖ Since it is the performance that drives readers theatre, children are given more opportunities to invest themselves and their personalities in the production of a readers theatre. The same story may be subject to several different presentations depending on the group or the individual youngsters involved. As such, children learn that readers theatre can be explored in a host of ways and a host of possibilities.

❖ Readers theatre is informal and relaxed. It does not require elaborate props, scenery, or costumes. It can be set up in any classroom or library. It does not require large sums of money to "make it happen." And, it can be "put on" in any kind of environment—formal or informal.

❖ Readers theatre stimulates the imagination and the creation of visual images. It has been substantiated that when youngsters are provided with opportunities to create their own mental images, their comprehension and appreciation of a piece of writing will be enhanced considerably. Since only a modicum of formal props and "set up" are required for any readers theatre production, the participants and audience are encouraged to create supplemental "props" in their minds—props that may be more elaborate and exquisite than those found in the most lavish of plays.

❖ Readers theatre enhances the development of cooperative learning strategies. It requires youngsters to work together toward a common goal and supports their efforts in doing so. Readers theatre is not a competitive activity, but rather a cooperative one in which children share, discuss, and band together for the good of the production.

❖ Teachers and librarians have also discovered that readers theatre is an excellent way in which to enhance the development of communication skills. Voice projection, intonation, inflection, and pronunciation skills are all promoted within and throughout any readers theatre production.

❖ The development and enhancement of self-concept is facilitated through readers theatre. Since children are working in concert with other children in a supportive atmosphere, their self-esteem mushrooms accordingly. Again, the emphasis is on the presentation, not necessarily the performers. As such, youngsters have opportunities to develop levels of self-confidence and self-assurance that would not normally be available in more traditional class productions.

❖ Creative and critical thinking are enhanced through the utilization of readers theatre. Children are active participants in the interpretation and delivery of a story; as such, they develop thinking skills that are divergent rather than convergent, and interpretive skills that are supported rather than directed.

❖ Readers theatre is fun! Children of all ages have delighted in using readers theatre for many years. It is delightful and stimulating, encouraging and fascinating, relevant and personal. Indeed, try as I might, I have not been able to locate a single instance (or group of children) in which (or for whom) readers theatre would not be an appropriate learning activity. It is a strategy filled with a cornucopia of possibilities and promises.

Readers theatre holds the promise of "energizing" your classroom language arts curriculum; stimulating your library program; and fostering an active and deeper engagement of students in all the dynamics of books, literature, and reading. For both classroom teachers and school librarians, its benefits are enormous and its implications endless.

READERS THEATRE AND THE READING/LANGUAGE ARTS STANDARDS

In response to a demand for a cohesive set of standards that address overall curriculum design and comprehensive student performance expectations in reading and language arts education, the International Reading Association, in concert with the National Council of Teachers of English, developed and promulgated the IRA/NCTE *Standards for the English Language Arts*. These standards provide a focused outline of the essential components of a well-structured language arts curriculum.

The 12 standards place an emphasis on literacy development as a lifelong process—one that starts well before youngsters enter school and continues throughout their lifetimes. Thus, these standards are intentionally integrative and multidisciplinary. Just as important, they support and underscore the values of readers theatre (see above) as a multipurpose language arts activity—one appropriate for both classroom and library.

The chart on page xiii provides an abridged and amended version of the English language arts standards. Along with each standard (as appropriate) is an explanation of how readers theatre serves as a valuable and innovative teaching tool in support of its corresponding standard.

English/Language Arts Standards*	Readers Theatre Support
1. Students are engaged in a wide variety of print and nonprint resources.	Readers theatre introduces students to a wealth of literature from a variety of cultural, historical, and literary sources.
2. Students are exposed to many genres of literature.	Readers theatre offers students a range of reading materials that span the 8 basic genres of children's literature.
3. Students use many reading strategies to comprehend text.	Readers theatre invites students to assume an active role in comprehension development through their engagement and participation.
4. Students communicate in a variety of ways.	Readers theatre invites students to practice reading, writing, listening, and speaking in an enjoyable and educative process.
5. Students learn through writing.	Readers theatre encourages students to develop their own scripts and share them with an audience.
6. Students use a variety of language conventions to understand text.	Readers theatre encourages students to discuss and understand how language conveys ideas.
7. Students are involved in personally meaningful research projects.	Readers theatre invites youngsters to examine and explore stories from a wide range of perspectives.
8. Students are comfortable with technology.	
9. Students gain an appreciation of language in a variety of venues.	Readers theatre encourages students to look at language and language use in a host of educational formats.
10. Non-English-speaking students develop competencies in all the language arts.	Readers theatre offers models of English use in a fun and engaging model.
11. Students are members of a host of literacy communities.	Readers theatre provides creative, investigative, and dynamic opportunities to see language in action.
12. Students use language for personal reasons.	Readers theatre offers innumerable opportunities for students to engage in personally enriching language activities.

*Modified and abridged from International Reading Association/National Council of Teachers of English, *Standards for the English Language Arts*, 1996.

When reviewing the standards, it should become evident that many elements of those standards can be promoted through the regular and systematic introduction of readers theatre into the elementary language arts curriculum. Equally important is the fact that those standards assist teachers and librarians in validating the impact and significance of readers theatre as a viable and valuable instructional tool—in language arts and throughout the entire elementary curriculum.

Please check out the two companion books: *Nonfiction Readers Theatre for Beginning Readers* and *Mother Goose Readers Theatre for Beginning Readers.*

Presentation Suggestions

It is important to remember that there is no single way to present readers theatre. What follows are some ideas you and the youngsters with whom you work may wish to keep in mind as you put on the productions in this book—whether in a classroom setting or the school library.

PREPARING SCRIPTS

One of the advantages of using readers theatre in the classroom is the lack of extra work or preparation time necessary to get "up and running." By using the scripts in this book, your preparation time is minimal.

❖ After a script has been selected for presentation, make sufficient copies. A copy of the script should be provided for each actor. In addition, two or three extra copies (one for you and "replacement" copies for scripts that are accidentally damaged or lost) are also a good idea. Copies for the audience are unnecessary and are not suggested.

❖ Each script can be bound between two sheets of colored construction paper or poster board. Bound scripts tend to formalize the presentation a little and lend an air of professionalism to the actors.

❖ Highlight each character's speaking parts with different color highlighter pens. This helps youngsters track their parts without being distracted by the dialogue of others.

STARTING OUT

Introducing the concept of readers theatre to your students for the first time may be as simple as sharing a script with the entire class and "walking" youngsters through the design and delivery of that script.

❖ Emphasize that a readers theatre performance does not require any memorization of the script. It's the interpretation and performance that count.

❖ You may wish to read through an entire script aloud, taking on the various roles. Let students know how easy and comfortable this process is.

❖ Encourage selected volunteers to read assigned parts of a sample script to the entire class. Readers should stand or sit in a circle so that other classmates can observe them.

❖ Provide opportunities for additional re-readings using other volunteers. Plan time to discuss the ease of presentation and the various interpretations offered by different readers.

❖ Readers should have an opportunity to practice their script before presenting it to an audience. Take some time to discuss voice intonation, facial gestures, body movements, and other features that could be used to enhance the presentation.

❖ Allow children the opportunity to suggest their own modifications, adaptations, or interpretations of the script. They will undoubtedly be "in tune" with the interests and perceptions of their peers and can offer some distinctive and personal interpretations.

❖ Encourage students to select nonstereotypical roles within any readers theatre script. For example, boys can take on female roles and girls can take on male roles, the smallest person in the class can take on the role of a giant dinosaur, or a shy student can take on the role of a boastful, bragging giant. Provide sufficient opportunities for students to expand and extend their appreciation of readers theatre through a variety of "out of character" roles.

STAGING

Staging involves the physical location of the readers as well as any necessary movements. Unlike a more formal play, the movements are often minimal. The emphasis is more on presentation and less on action.

❖ For most presentations, readers will stand or sit on stools or chairs. The physical location of each reader has been indicated for each of the scripts in this book.

❖ If there are many characters in the presentation, it may be advantageous to have characters in the rear (upstage) standing while those in the front (downstage) are placed on stools or chairs. This ensures that the audience will both see and hear each actor.

❖ Usually all of the characters will be on stage throughout the duration of the presentation. For most presentations it is not necessary to have characters enter and exit the presentation. If you place the characters on stools, they can face the audience when they are involved in a particular scene and then turn around whenever they are not involved in a scene.

❖ You may wish to make simple hand-lettered signs with the name of each character. Loop a piece of string or yarn through each sign and hang it around the neck of each respective character. That way, the audience will know the identity of each character throughout the presentation.

❖ Each reader will have her or his own copy of the script in a paper cover (see above). If possible, use a music stand for each reader's script (this allows readers to use their hands for dramatic interpretation as necessary).

❖ Several presentations have a narrator to set up the story. The narrator serves to establish the place and time of the story for the audience so that the characters can "jump into" their parts from the beginning of the story. Typically, the narrator is separated from the other "actors" and can be identified by a simple sign.

PROPS

Two of the positive features of readers theatre are its ease of preparation and its ease of presentation. Informality is a hallmark of any readers theatre script.

❖ Much of the setting for a story should take place in the audience's mind. Elaborate scenery is not necessary—simple props are often the best. For example:

    – A branch or potted plant may serve as a tree.

    – A drawing on the chalkboard may illustrate a building.

    – A hand-lettered sign may designate one part of the staging area as a particular scene (e.g., swamp, castle, field, forest).

    – Children's toys may be used for uncomplicated props (e.g., telephone, vehicles).

- A sheet of aluminum foil or a remnant of blue cloth may be used to simulate a lake or pond.

❖ Costumes for the actors are unnecessary. A few simple items may be suggested by students. For example:

- Hats, scarves, or aprons may be used by major characters.

- A paper cutout may serve as a tie, button, or badge.

- Old clothing (borrowed from parents) may be used as warranted.

❖ Some teachers and librarians have discovered that the addition of appropriate background music or sound effects enhances a readers theatre presentation.

❖ It's important to remember that the emphasis in readers theatre is on the reading—not on any accompanying "features." The best presentations are often the simplest.

DELIVERY

I've often found it advantageous to let students know that the only difference between a readers theatre presentation and a movie role is that they will have a script in their hands. This allows them to focus more on presenting rather than memorizing a script.

❖ When first introduced to readers theatre, students often have a tendency to "read into" their scripts. Encourage students to look up from their scripts and interact with other characters or the audience as necessary

❖ Practicing the script beforehand can eliminate the problem of students burying their heads in the pages. In so doing, children understand the need to involve the audience as much as possible in the development of the story.

❖ Voice projection and delivery are important in allowing the audience to understand characters' actions. The proper mood and intent needs to be established—which is possible when children are familiar and comfortable with each character's "style."

❖ Again, the emphasis is on delivery, so be sure to suggest different types of voice (e.g., angry, irritated, calm, frustrated, excited) that children may wish to use for their particular character(s).

POST-PRESENTATION

As a wise author once said, "The play's the thing." So it is with readers theatre. In other words, the mere act of presenting a readers theatre script is complete in and of itself. It is not necessary, or even required, to do any type of formalized evaluation after readers theatre. Once again, the emphasis is on informality. Readers theatre should and can be a pleasurable and stimulating experience for children.

What follows are a few ideas you may want to share with students. In doing so, you will be providing youngsters with important learning opportunities that extend and promote all aspects of your reading and language arts program.

❖ After a presentation, discuss with students how the script enhanced or altered the original story.

❖ Invite students to suggest other characters who could be added to the script.

- ❖ Invite students to suggest new or alternate dialogue for various characters

- ❖ Invite students to suggest new or different setting(s) for the script.

- ❖ Invite students to talk about their reactions to various characters' expressions, tone of voice, presentations, or dialogues.

- ❖ After a presentation, invite youngsters to suggest any modifications or changes needed in the script.

Presenting a readers theatre script need not be an elaborate or extensive production. As children become more familiar with and polished in using readers theatre, they will be able to suggest a multitude of presentation possibilities for future scripts. It is important to help children assume a measure of self-initiated responsibility in the delivery of any readers theatre. In so doing, you will be helping to ensure their personal engagement and active participation in this most valuable of language arts activities.

Bonus Features

This resource has been especially designed for classroom teachers, school librarians, or reading specialists who work with beginning readers; specifically youngsters in grades K–2. Teaching children in these grades has always been a challenge, yet the opportunities for literacy growth and development are enormous. Readers theatre has proven itself as one way you can help children learn language in context in addition to enhancing your overall reading or language arts program.

To help make your task of teaching primary-level youngsters a little easier, several bonus features have been included throughout the book. Please consider these as important elements in the introduction and use of readers theatre in your classroom or library.

READABILITY

Each of the scripts in this book has been assessed according to its readability—or its appropriateness for a specific reading grade level. You will discover 24 scripts written at the both the first- and second-grade levels. The primary factors in determining the readability of a script were sentence length and average number of syllables per word. With this in mind, you will be able to use scripts that are appropriate for an entire class as well as selected individuals within a class.

MUSICAL VERSIONS

For each of the scripts in this book I have provided you with a Web site that has a recorded musical version of the selected song/rhyme. The ease of access to the Internet and the easy availability of recordings makes these ideal resources for most classroom teachers and school librarians. Please note that the songs in this book, and the musical versions recommended for each readers theatre script, are all in the public domain—that is, they are copyright free.

You are encouraged to play the selected songs through your computer. Many of the songs repeat themselves over and over—thus providing youngsters with a continuous version of a song and an easy way to learn the rhyme, tempo, and beat of a selected song. You may, of course, wish to play each selected song one or two times only.

Following are some of the best Web sites for children's songs—those in this book as well as others you may wish to use in your classroom or library:

❖ **http://www.niehs.nih.gov/kids/music.htm#index**—This Web site is monitored by the National Institutes of Health, Department of Health & Human Services. It has one of the most complete and extensive collections of children's song lyrics and music I have ever encountered. More than 400 midi files and lyrics are catalogued on this site, from classics ("Do Your Ears Hang Low?") to contemporary ("Forrest Gump Theme Song"). Also included is information about copyrights and how to access the musical files.

❖ **http://www.kididdles.com/**—This commercial Web site has an eclectic collection of children's songs as well as other classroom activities and games. It offers both music and lyrics for some of the most popular and most familiar classroom songs.

- ❖ **http://www.theteachersguide.com/ChildrensSongs.htm**—Here is another commercial site that has a varied collection of both lyrics and midis for classroom and library use. The links are easy to access and easy to use.

- ❖ **http://www.bussongs.com/**—This site was created to help kids, parents, and teachers recall the words to familiar songs that bring back warm memories of field trips, family reunions, and summer camp. The site also includes some lullabies and nursery rhymes.

The music that accompanies each of the songs in this book can be used in a variety of ways. Here are some suggestions I've found to be particularly helpful:

- ❖ Play the midi files for children several times before the actual presentation. This helps them become familiar with the rhyme and rhythm of the music.

- ❖ Play the applicable midi file as a follow-up to any script you share with youngsters. Plan time to discuss any similarities between the recorded version and the version they "produced" in the classroom of library.

- ❖ Have the accompanying midi file playing softly in the background as a script is being shared with the class.

- ❖ Teach children the words to a song first, then invite them to listen to the words with the accompanying midi file. Afterward invite them to share the related script.

- ❖ Use the words in a song as part of a vocabulary lesson. You may wish to teach the words in context or as individual vocabulary words.

- ❖ Listen carefully to the language used by children in everyday situations. Take advantage of that language and incorporate it into personalized versions of familiar songs.

- ❖ Just like readers theatre, song-related activities work best when they are promoted as group-based activities. Lots of interaction among students is the key to their success.

- ❖ Don't limit songs and rhymes to a specific time of the day, but rather take advantage of the unplanned and informal opportunities that arise naturally (those "teachable moments"). Times when children line up for lunch, story time, indoor recess, and "Show and Tell" time are but a few of the many opportunities you'll have to include some playful language activities.

As you are aware, the Internet is extremely volatile. That is, it is always changing and always evolving. The Web sites listed above (and others you may locate via a search engine) may change over time. At the time of the writing of this book, the sites listed above were active and easily accessible. Please be aware that there may be some changes by the time you read this book; however, I have tried to provide you with four sites that seem to have some degree of permanency.

TEACHING OPTIONS

To help you share the music of these songs with students in your classroom or library program, you may wish to consider the following options:

- ❖ Invite the school music teacher to prepare a set of cassette or CD recordings of selected tunes. She or he may have prerecorded versions available as part of the music library. The music teacher may also be willing to record selected songs for you on an "as needed" basis.

From *Songs and Rhymes Readers Theatre for Beginning Readers* by Anthony D. Fredericks. Westport, CT: Teacher Ideas Press. Copyright © 2008.

❖ Check with a local teacher supply store or music store to see what types of recordings of children's songs they may have in stock. I have found many recordings of popular children's songs at a local branch of Borders or Barnes & Noble.

❖ If you, a relative, or a friend has some musical talent, you may wish to create your own versions of popular songs. Children will be particularly responsive to recordings made by their teacher or librarian or someone else with whom they are familiar.

❖ You may know of parents who would be willing to create some recordings of selected songs.

❖ You may wish to ask a local band to make a few recordings of selected songs. (They may be willing to do this as part of a community service effort.) Contact the music director at the local high school for assistance in finding some local talent.

❖ Contact your local public library to see what types of recorded children's songs it has in its collection. I recently contacted the public library system in the county in which I live and discovered 677 audiorecordings (cassette tapes and CDs) of various collections of children's songs in the system. *Note:* At the end of this section I have provided you with a very brief bibliography of some popular song collections that you may wish to check out from your local library, bookstore, online bookseller (e.g. Amazon.com), or catalogs of publishers of children's music (available through your school's music teacher).

MOVEMENT/DANCE

The scripts in this book provide you with opportunities to help students understand the role of language arts as an active learning opportunity. Students are encouraged to speak, listen, read, and write in a host of mutually satisfying endeavors that promote and extend language as not just a "school-based" subject, but also one in which they can experience success and enjoyment.

Thus, in addition to the musical accompaniments to the scripts in this book, there are also suggestions for movement and dance. These activities may be related directly to the song, directly to the script, or both. While these may be viewed as optional activities, I would like to suggest that you consider many of them as a regular and necessary part of your overall language arts program. By doing so, you will be helping children appreciate the active participation that underscores effective language learning as well as the fun that can be part of any learning opportunity.

Here are a few considerations:

❖ The suggested movement or dance for each script is listed separately from the script. You may wish to present it to children apart from the script (either before or after) or as an element of the overall production.

❖ In some cases, the movement or dance has been incorporated into the script. Performers, as well as the audience, may be asked to engage in some movement activities as part of the overall script.

❖ You may wish to have a small group of students perform the movement or dance while another group performs the script.

❖ After students are comfortable presenting movement or dance activities, invite them to make suggestions for other types of interpretations (other than those in this book). Tap into students' creative wisdom by encouraging them to develop their own movement or dance "productions."

❖ Students may wish to share some of their movement or dance activities with another class. You may wish to make arrangements with another teacher for a special sharing day of selected songs.

From *Songs and Rhymes Readers Theatre for Beginning Readers* by Anthony D. Fredericks. Westport, CT: Teacher Ideas Press. Copyright © 2008.

❖ Consider these suggestions as either individual or group activities. One or two students, or an entire class, are encouraged to practice and share their dances.

The movement or dance activities included in this book have been developed in cooperation with many primary level teachers and librarians. Although they are presented in concert with selected scripts, you are certainly encouraged to use them as separate learning activities. When students begin to understand the natural connections that can exist between language learning and physical activity, their appreciation of readers theatre as a valuable and viable learning tool will mushroom exponentially.

Bibliography

COLLECTIONS OF RECORDED CHILDREN'S MUSIC (CDS AND CASSETTES)

A very brief bibliography.

Best of Children's Favorites. Burbank, CA: Walt Disney Records, 2004.

Best Toddler Tunes. Swanton, VT: Kidzup, 1999.

Capon, Jack. *Children's All-Time Rhythm Favorites.* Freeport, NY: Activity Records, 1987.

Countdown Kids. *50 All-Time Children's Favorites.* St. Laurent, QC: Madacy Entertainment, 2000.

Countdown Kids. *Mary Has a Little Lamb.* St. Laurent, QC: Madacy Entertainment, 1998.

Favorite Children's Songs. New York: Sony Music, 2004.

Learning Station. *All-Time Children's Favorites.* Melbourne, FL: Kaladon Publishing, 1999.

McGrath, Bob. *If You're Happy and You Know It.* Teaneck, NJ: Bob's Kids Music, 1996.

Mother Goose Songbook. Emeryville, CA: Leapfrog School House, 2001.

Nelson, Esther. *Sing, Dance, Listen.* Bronx, NY: Dimension 5, 1987.

Old McDonald and Other Favorites. Norwalk, CT: Studio Mouse, 2002.

Raffi. *Celebration of Family.* Los Angeles: Kid Rhino, 2001.

———. *A Child's Celebration of Lullaby.* Redway, CA: Music for Little People, 1997.

———. *More Singable Songs.* Vancouver, BC: Shoreline Records, 1977.

———. *Singable Songs for the Very Young.* Cambridge, MA: Rounder, 1996.

Sharon, Lois. *Mainly Mother Goose.* Los Angeles: Elephant Records, 1994.

RELATED READERS THEATRE BOOKS

Fredericks, Anthony D. *African Legends, Myths, and Folktales for Readers Theatre.* Westport, CT: Teacher Ideas Press, 2008.

———. *Frantic Frogs and Other Frankly Fractured Folktales for Readers Theatre.* Westport, CT: Teacher Ideas Press, 1993.

———. *MORE Frantic Frogs and Other Frankly Fractured Folktales for Readers Theatre.* Westport, CT: Teacher Ideas Press, 2008.

———. *Mother Goose Readers Theatre for Beginning Readers.* Westport, CT: Teacher Ideas Press, 2007.

———. *Nonfiction Readers Theatre for Beginning Readers.* Westport, CT: Teacher Ideas Press, 2007.

————. *Readers Theatre for American History.* Westport, CT: Teacher Ideas Press, 2001.

————. *Science Fiction Readers Theatre.* Westport, CT: Teacher Ideas Press, 2002.

————. *Silly Salamanders and Other Slightly Stupid Stories for Readers Theatre.* Westport, CT: Teacher Ideas Press, 2000.

————. *Tadpole Tales and Other Totally Terrific Treats for Readers Theatre.* Westport, CT: Teacher Ideas Press, 1997.

Songs and Rhymes Readers Theatre for Beginning Readers

Mary Had a Little Lamb

PRESENTATION SUGGESTIONS

The script uses the lyrics for the song embedded inside the story. During the reading of the lyrics, you may wish to play the music in the background, although this is not required. Or after the presentation you may wish to teach the entire class the lyrics to the song and invite them to sing along with the music.

PROPS

If possible obtain a stuffed lamb or sheep to place in the middle of the staging area. You may wish to project a picture of a lamb or sheep on the wall behind the players or display farm scenes from your picture files.

DELIVERY

The characters should all be concerned and slightly worried about Mary. Mary should talk in a pleasant voice. The narrator should deliver her or his lines in a serious tone.

MUSICAL VERSION

Log on to the following Web site for an easy-to-follow musical rendition of this popular nursery rhyme: http://www.niehs.nih.gov/kids/lyrics/mary.htm.

MOVEMENT/DANCE

Here is an activity all students can participate in after watching the readers theatre production. Place the students in one large circle or in several smaller circles. After students are comfortable with the various movements, add the music to this activity.

Mary had a little lamb,
["Walk" fingers of one hand over the palm of the other hand.]
Little lamb, little lamb,
["Walk" fingers of one hand over the palm of the other hand.]
Mary had a little lamb,
["Walk" fingers of one hand over the palm of the other hand.]
Its fleece was white as snow.

And everywhere that Mary went,
[Walk in a counterclockwise circle.]
Mary went, Mary went,
[Walk in a counterclockwise circle.]
Everywhere that Mary went,
[Walk in a counterclockwise circle.]
The lamb was sure to go.

It followed her to school one day,
[Continue walking; place right hand on shoulder of person in front.]
School one day, school one day,
[Continue walking; place right hand on shoulder of person in front.]
It followed her to school one day,
[Continue walking; place right hand on shoulder of person in front.]
Which was a gainst the rules.

It made the children laugh and play,
[Simulate laughing while continuing to walk in circle.]
Laugh and play, laugh and play,
[Simulate laughing while continuing to walk in circle.]
It made the children laugh and play,
[Simulate laughing while continuing to walk in circle.]
To see a lamb at school.

Mary Had a Little Lamb

STAGING: The narrator can sit on a stool or stand at a lectern on the side of the staging area. The characters should all be standing in a loose-knit group. They can occasionally move around as they are speaking to one another.

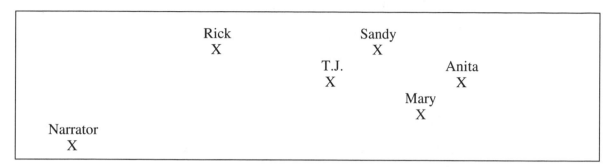

NARRATOR: Good day, everybody. My friends [points to characters] and I have a story to tell.

MARY: Yes, it's a story about me.

NARRATOR: That's right. Our friend [points to Mary] got into trouble.

MARY: That's right. I got into trouble.

NARRATOR: Let's share your story. Let's go.

RICK: Yeah, one day, we were all at school.

SANDY: Some of us were playing soccer.

T.J.: And some were playing baseball.

ANITA: We were waiting for school to begin.

SANDY: Finally, the bell rang.

RICK: And we all lined up.

T.J.: Our teacher was there. She told us to go inside.

SANDY: Then we saw Mary.

ANITA: She was walking up the road.

T.J.: There was something following her.

From *Songs and Rhymes Readers Theatre for Beginning Readers* by Anthony D. Fredericks. Westport, CT: Teacher Ideas Press. Copyright © 2008.

RICK: It was her pet lamb, "Boo Boo."

SANDY: She didn't see the lamb behind her.

ANITA: Mary was running to get to school. She didn't see the lamb behind her.

T.J.: Our teacher stopped her.

ANITA: The teacher said she couldn't bring a lamb to school.

MARY: I didn't know what she was talking about.

T.J.: So, I told her to turn around.

MARY: When I turned around there was Boo-Boo.

ANITA: I think Mary was surprised.

MARY: Yes, I was surprised.

RICK: The teacher told her she couldn't have the lamb.

MARY: So I told her that I didn't know Boo-Boo followed me.

ANITA: I think the teacher was angry.

MARY: Yes, the teacher was very angry. She said a lamb can't come to school.

RICK: Mary didn't know what to do.

SANDY: Mary was thinking. All the students were laughing.

ANITA: Yes, everybody was laughing.

MARY: I didn't know what to do.

RICK: The teacher was getting more angry.

T.J.: She said Mary had to take the lamb home.

MARY: The teacher told me to take the lamb home. Then she said I could come back to school.

SANDY: All the other students were still laughing.

RICK: Everybody thought it was very funny.

T.J.: Then, Mary had an idea.

MARY: Yes, I asked her if Boo-Boo could stay on the playground.

ANITA: The teacher thought about that.

RICK: Then she said that the lamb could stay. The lamb could stay and eat the grass.

SANDY: Everybody laughed and laughed. They thought this was very funny.

MARY: It was a funny day. My lamb came to school. And, my lamb stayed at school the whole day.

T.J.: Somebody from the newspaper came to school. He saw the lamb. He talked to Mary. He talked to the teacher. He talked to all the students.

ANITA: And then he wrote about Mary's lamb.

MARY: Yes, he wrote a song about Boo-Boo.

RICK: It's a good song.

T.J.: We'd like to sing the song for you.

SANDY: Is everybody ready? OK, here goes.

RICK: Mary had a little lamb,

SANDY: Little lamb, little lamb,

T.J.: Mary had a little lamb,

ANITA: Its fleece was white as snow.

RICK: And everywhere that Mary went,

SANDY: Mary went, Mary went,

T.J.: Everywhere that Mary went,

ANITA: The lamb was sure to go.

RICK: It followed her to school one day,

SANDY: School one day, school one day,

T.J.: It followed her to school one day,

ANITA: Which was against the rules.

RICK: It made the children laugh and play,

SANDY: Laugh and play, laugh and play,

T.J.: It made the children laugh and play,

ANITA: To see a lamb at school.

MARY: And that's the end of my story. And that's the end of our song.

Twinkle, Twinkle Little Star

PRESENTATION SUGGESTIONS

Plan to introduce the music for this rhyme (see below) prior to the presentation. The audience can then join the characters in singing the song during the last portion of the presentation.

PROPS

You may wish to cut a large star from a piece of construction paper. Hang the star from the ceiling or a light fixture. Encourage the characters to point to the star periodically throughout the production.

DELIVERY

The characters should be having a friendly and enjoyable conversation. The tone is light and comfortable.

MUSICAL VERSION

Log on to the following Web site (or a similar piece of recorded music): http://www. kinderplanet.com/twinkles.htm.

As soon as the page loads, the song "Twinkle, Twinkle, Little Star" will begin to play (the site repeats the song over and over). Students may wish to follow the lyrics on the screen (they are identical to those used in the following script).

MOVEMENT/DANCE

This is a song that can be "performed" by everyone in the class. Invite all students to stand in a large circle. Teach them the movements below for each line of the lyrics. When students are sufficiently practiced, play the music, sing the song, and do all the movements simultaneously.

Twinkle, twinkle, little star,
[Put both hands in the air; wriggle all fingers.]
How I wonder what you are,
[Stroke chin as though thinking.]
Up above the world so high,
[Point upward with one finger.]
Like a diamond in the sky.
[Put hands loosely together; alternately tap fingers together in a rapid motion.]
Twinkle, twinkle little star,
[Put both hands in the air; wiggle all fingers.]
How I wonder what you are.
[Stroke chin as though thinking.]

[Repeat.]

Twinkle, Twinkle Little Star

STAGING: The characters should all be standing in a loose circle. Occasionally they will look upwards and/or point upwards (as if gazing at a star or other celestial body).

Narrator			
X			
	Rick	Diane	Karen
	X	X	X

NARRATOR: Once upon a time there were three friends.

RICK: That's me!

DIANE: And me!

KAREN: And me!

NARRATOR: That's right! Well, one day they went for a walk.

RICK: That's right, we went for a walk.

DIANE: Don't forget the most important thing.

RICK: What's that?

KAREN: We went for a walk at night.

RICK: That's right. Now I remember.

NARRATOR: While they were walking someone looked up.

DIANE: That would be me.

KAREN: Yes, Diane looked up.

RICK: That's right.

NARRATOR: Anyway, when Diane looked up she saw something.

DIANE: Yes, I saw something.

RICK: I know what she saw.

From *Songs and Rhymes Readers Theatre for Beginning Readers* by Anthony D. Fredericks. Westport, CT: Teacher Ideas Press. Copyright © 2008.

KAREN: So do I!

NARRATOR: [points to audience] And you do, too!

DIANE: When I looked up I saw a little star.

KAREN: It was a tiny star.

RICK: It was a little itsy bitsy star!

DIANE: I didn't know what it was at first.

KAREN: So I looked at it, too.

RICK: And so did I.

DIANE: While we looked at it, it began to twinkle.

RICK: What does that mean?

KAREN: It means that the star was shining.

DIANE: And it means that the star was blinking.

RICK: Yeah, a shining and blinking star.

DIANE: It was very, very bright!

KAREN: Really, really bright.

RICK: It was as bright as a diamond.

DIANE: It looked like a very bright diamond.

KAREN: My mother has a diamond ring. It sparkles and shines.

DIANE: This star was sparkling and shining, too.

NARRATOR: The three friends had an idea.

RICK: Yes, we had an idea.

KAREN: Yes, we had a great idea!

DIANE: It was a brilliant idea!

NARRATOR: They decided to write a song. A song just for you [points to audience].

RICK: We'd like to sing our song.

DIANE: Yes, we will sing our song for you.

KAREN: And maybe you may want to sing it, too.

RICK: Are you ready? Here we go!

DIANE: Twinkle, twinkle, little star,

KAREN: How I wonder what you are,

RICK: Up above the world so high,

DIANE: Like a diamond in the sky.

KAREN: Twinkle, twinkle, little star,

RICK: How I wonder what you are!

NARRATOR: Please do it one more time. This time the audience [points] can join in. Are you ready? Here goes!

DIANE: Twinkle, twinkle, little star,

KAREN: How I wonder what you are,

RICK: Up above the world so high,

DIANE: Like a diamond in the sky.

KAREN: Twinkle, twinkle, little star,

RICK: How I wonder what you are!

NARRATOR: And that's the end!

The Itsy Bitsy Spider

PRESENTATION SUGGESTIONS

This script should be shared with students in advance of the singing of the song. You may wish to teach the song to the players in this readers theatre production and then invite them to teach it to their classmates. After sufficient practice, invite your students to consider sharing the production and song with another class.

PROPS

You may wish to post several photographs of various spider species around the room in advance of this production. If possible place a large plastic spider on a stool in the middle of the staging area.

DELIVERY

The characters are all inquisitive. The narrator takes on the persona of a teacher as she or he provides the important information about spiders.

MUSICAL VERSION

Log on to the following Web site for a lively version of this ever-popular song: http://www.niehs.nih.gov/kids/lyrics/spider.htm.

MOVEMENT/DANCE

Invite all students to learn the movements associated with this song. You will quickly discover, as have I, that youngsters love "performing" this song (and the accompanying movements) with or without the music. They will want to "do" the song many times throughout the day.

The itsy bitsy spider,
[Place right little finger on left thumb, twist hands around in order to place right
thumb on left litle finger, twist hands again to place right little finger on left thumb,
and continue in upward motion.]
Crawled up the water spout.
[Repeat as above.]

Down came the rain,
[Hands over head, bring down quickly.]
And washed the spider out.
[Move hands outward at bottom of movement.]

Out came the sun,
[Hold arms in large circle over head.]
And dried up all the rain.
[Hands below waist, raise upward while wiggling fingers.]

And the itsy bitsy spider
[Place right little finger on left thumb, twist hands around in order to place right thumb
on left litle finger, twist hands again to place right little finger on left thumb, and continue
in upward motion.]
Crawled up the spout again.
[Repeat as above.]

The Itsy Bitsy Spider

STAGING: The narrator can sit on a stool in front of and to the side of all the characters. The characters may wish to stand and physically interact with each other or sit on chairs or stools.

```
                    Steve           Elizabeth
                     X                  X         Troy
                                                   X
           Rajean
            X                    LaToya
                                   X
   Narrator
    X
```

NARRATOR: [to characters] Welcome to science class. [to class] Welcome to science class.

STEVE: What are we going to learn?

NARRATOR: We are going to learn about spiders.

ELIZABETH: I like spiders.

TROY: So do I.

RAJEAN: I think spiders are icky.

LATOYA: Me, too.

NARRATOR: Well, spiders are amazing animals.

STEVE: What do you mean?

NARRATOR: Well, there are many kinds of spiders.

ELIZABETH: How many?

NARRATOR: There are more than 35,000 different kinds.

TROY: Wow, that's a lot of spiders!

NARRATOR: Yes, and spiders live all over the world.

RAJEAN: Even in my house?

From *Songs and Rhymes Readers Theatre for Beginning Readers* by Anthony D. Fredericks. Westport, CT: Teacher Ideas Press. Copyright © 2008.

NARRATOR: Yes, you could have spiders in your house.

LATOYA: Yuck, that sounds creepy.

NARRATOR: No, it isn't. Spiders help us.

STEVE: How do spiders help us?

NARRATOR: They eat insects.

ELIZABETH: That sounds gross!

NARRATOR: Not really. Spider eat dangerous insects. They eat insects that might hurt us. They eat insects that carry disease.

TROY: I guess spiders are good for us.

NARRATOR: Yes, they are.

RAJEAN: What else do you know about spiders?

NARRATOR: All spiders have 8 legs.

LATOYA: I didn't know that.

NARRATOR: That's right. Spiders have 8 legs. All insects have 6 legs.

STEVE: So, that means that spiders are different from insects.

NARRATOR: That's right!

ELIZABETH: Hey, this is pretty interesting.

NARRATOR: Yes it is. Here's something else—spiders have 8 eyes.

ALL: EIGHT EYES!!!

NARRATOR: That's right. All spiders have 8 eyes. Their eyes are different from our eyes. We have 2 eyes. Spiders have 8 eyes.

TROY: Spiders must look weird.

NARRATOR: I guess they do. You have to look real hard to see all their eyes.

RAJEAN: I'm glad I don't have 8 eyes.

LATOYA: What kind of glasses would you wear if you had 8 eyes?

NARRATOR: Here's something else. Some spiders can fly.

ALL: FLY!!!

NARRATOR: Well, not fly like a bird.

STEVE: Can they fly like a butterfly?

ELIZABETH: Or like a bumblebee?

TROY: Or like an airplane?

NARRATOR: Well, no. Some spiders spin silk. They make a long silk line. The wind blows the line up in the air. The spider hangs on. It goes for a ride. It can travel a long way.

RAJEAN: Wow, that sounds neat!

LATOYA: I wish I could do that.

STEVE: Wouldn't that be cool?

ELIZABETH: It sure would.

TROY: Hey, you know what? Spiders are really cool.

RAJEAN: They're really neat!

LATOYA: Yeah, I think I like spiders now.

STEVE: Me, too.

ELIZABETH: And me, too!

TROY: [to narrator] What else can you tell us?

NARRATOR: Well, there is a song about a spider.

RAJEAN: Is it a fun song?

LATOYA: Is it as fun as spiders.

NARRATOR: Yes, it is. So, would you like to sing it?

ALL: YES!!!

NARRATOR: Then, let's go.

[Play the music and invite the entire class to sing the song. Encourage them to use the accompanying movements as indicated above.]

The Farmer in the Dell

PRESENTATION SUGGESTIONS

The song "Farmer in the Dell" is embedded in this script. You may wish to play the music for this song several times so that students are used to the pattern and pace of the music. As children become more practiced, they may wish to perform the script with the accompanying music.

PROPS

There are no props necessary for this script. However, if you wish you may want to set up a small table in the middle of the staging area with small toy animals or stuffed animals (the ones in the song) placed on the table. As each character says her or his lines, she or he can hold up the appropriate animal from the table.

DELIVERY

The lines should all be delivered as though they might be sung in a song. You may wish to practice the song with students in advance of any presentation.

MUSICAL VERSION

Log on to the following Web site for a sprightly rendition of this all-time popular song: http://www.niehs.nih.gov/kids/lyrics/farmer.htm.

MOVEMENT/DANCE

Arrange all the students in a large circle. Place one student (the Farmer) in the center of the circle. Begin the music, start singing the song, and have the children move in a counterclockwise rotation. At the end of the second verse, the Farmer chooses a Wife (any individual from the circle), who joins him in the middle of the circle. At the end of the third verse, the Wife takes a Child (any individual from the circle). At the end of the fourth verse, the Child takes a Nurse, and so on. The last person to enter the circle is the Cheese. And then the last verse is sung by everybody.

The farmer in the dell,
[Everyone sings.]
The farmer in the dell,
Hi-ho, the derry-o,
The farmer in the dell.

The farmer takes a wife,
[Wife enters the circle.]
The farmer takes a wife,
Hi-ho, the derry-o,
The farmer takes a wife.

The wife takes a child,
[Child enters the circle.]
The wife takes a child,
Hi-ho, the derry-o,
The wife takes a child.

The child takes a nurse,
[Nurse enters the circle.]
The child takes a nurse,
Hi-ho, the derry-o,
The child takes a nurse.

The nurse takes a cow,
[Cow enters the circle.]
The nurse takes a cow,
Hi-ho, the derry-o,
The nurse takes a cow.

The cow takes a dog,
[Dog enters the circle.]
The cow takes a dog,
Hi-ho, the derry-o,
The cow takes a dog.

The dog takes a cat,
[Cat enters the circle.]
The dog takes a cat,
Hi-ho, the derry-o,
The dog takes a cat.

The cat takes a rat,
[Rat enters the circle.]
The cat takes a rat,
Hi-ho, the derry-o,
The cat takes a rat.

The rat takes the cheese,
[Cheese enters the circle.]
The rat takes the cheese,
Hi-ho, the derry-o,
The rat takes the cheese.

The cheese stands alone,
[Everyone but the cheese leaves the circle.]
The cheese stands alone,
Hi-ho, the derry-o,
The cheese stands alone.

The farmer in the dell,
[Everyone sings.]
The farmer in the dell,
Hi-ho, the derry-o,
The farmer in the dell.

The Farmer in the Dell

STAGING: The characters can all be scattered about the staging area. They may be seated on stools or chairs. There is no narrator for this script.

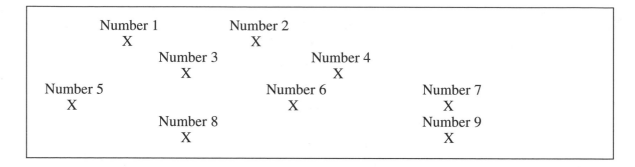

NUMBER 1: We're going to tell you about a farmer.

NUMBER 2: He has a lot of animals.

NUMBER 3: Some animals are big.

NUMBER 4: Some animals are small.

NUMBER 5: Some animals are hairy.

NUMBER 6: And some animals are funny.

NUMBER 7: But they are all nice animals.

NUMBER 8: And they all live on the farm.

NUMBER 9: Which stinks sometimes!

NUMBER 1: We're going to need your help.

NUMBER 2: We need you to help us tell our story.

NUMBER 3: We need you to say some things.

NUMBER 4: It will make the story more fun.

NUMBER 5: We'll say some stuff, too.

NUMBER 6: So, everyone will have a part in this story.

NUMBER 7: We hope you're ready for some fun.

NUMBER 8: Are you ready?

NUMBER 9: Here we go.

ALL: The farmer in the dell,

ALL: The farmer in the dell,

ALL: Hi-ho, the derry-o,

ALL: The farmer in the dell.

NUMBER 1: The farmer takes a wife,

ALL: The farmer takes a wife,

AUDIENCE: Hi-ho, the derry-o,

NUMBER 1: The farmer takes a wife.

NUMBER 2: The wife takes a child,

ALL: The wife takes a child,

AUDIENCE: Hi-ho, the derry-o,

NUMBER 2: The wife takes a child.

NUMBER 3: The child takes a nurse,

ALL: The child takes a nurse,

AUDIENCE: Hi-ho, the derry-o,

NUMBER 3: The child takes a nurse.

NUMBER 4: The nurse takes a cow,

ALL: The nurse takes a cow,

AUDIENCE: Hi-ho, the derry-o,

NUMBER 4: The nurse takes a cow.

NUMBER 5: The cow takes a dog,

ALL: The cow takes a dog,

AUDIENCE: Hi-ho, the derry-o,

NUMBER 5: The cow takes a dog.

NUMBER 6: The dog takes a cat,

ALL: The dog takes a cat,

AUDIENCE: Hi-ho, the derry-o,

NUMBER 6: The dog takes a cat.

NUMBER 7: The cat takes a rat,

ALL: The cat takes a rat,

AUDIENCE: Hi-ho, the derry-o,

NUMBER 7: The cat takes a rat.

NUMBER 8: The rat takes the cheese,

ALL: The rat takes the cheese,

AUDIENCE: Hi-ho, the derry-o,

NUMBER 8: The rat takes the cheese.

NUMBER 9: The cheese stands alone,

ALL: The cheese stands alone,

AUDIENCE: Hi-ho, the derry-o,

NUMBER 9: The cheese stands alone.

ALL: The farmer in the dell,

ALL: The farmer in the dell,

ALL: Hi-ho, the derry-o,

ALL: The famer in the dell.

NUMBER 1: You did a very good job.

NUMBER 2: Yes, you helped us a lot.

NUMBER 3: That was a lot of fun!

NUMBER 4: Thank you for all your work.

NUMBER 5: It's time to stop now.

NUMBER 6: We have to go.

NUMBER 7: Our story is done.

NUMBER 8: We are finished.

NUMBER 9: We are done!

ALL: Good-bye!

Polly Wolly Doodle
All the Day

PRESENTATION SUGGESTIONS

In this script you, the teacher, play a major role. You will accompany the three singers in this readers theatre presentation. Please note that the entire script is the entire song "Polly Wolly Doodle All the Day."

PROPS

No props are necessary for this presentation.

DELIVERY

As a major character you may wish to present your lines as though you were reading them. Or you may wish to sing your lines (with or without the accompanying music). The singers should also have the same option—reading their lines or singing them along with the music.

MUSICAL VERSION

Log on to the following Web site for a lively and quick-tempoed version of this fun-to-sing song: http://www.niehs.nih.gov/kids/lyrics/polly.htm.

MOVEMENT/DANCE

Arrange all the students in a large circle. Play the music and invite them to move and sing according to the following directions (be prepared for lots of fun and hilarity):

Oh, I went down South for to see my Sal,
[Walk counterclockwise in circle.]
Sing Polly wolly doodle all the day. [Stop.]
My Sal, she is a spunky gal,
[Walk clockwise in circle.]
Sing Polly wolly doodle all the day. [Stop.]

Fare thee well, [Clap, clap.] fare thee well, [Clap, clap.]
Fare thee well my fairy fay, [Clap, clap.]
For I'm going to Lou'siana for to see my Susyanna.
Sing Polly wolly doodle all the day. [Clap, clap.]

Oh, my Sal, she is a maiden fair,
[Walk counterclockwise in circle.]
Sing Polly wolly doodle all the day. [Stop.]
With curly eyes and laughing hair,
[Walk clockwise in circle.]
Sing Polly wolly doodle all the day. [Stop.]

Fare thee well, [Clap, clap.] fare thee well, [Clap, clap.]
Fare thee well my fairy fay, [Clap, clap.]
For I'm going to Lou'siana for to see my Susyanna,
Sing Polly wolly doodle all the day. [Clap, clap.]

Behind the barn, down on my knees,
[Walk counterclockwise in circle.]
Sing Polly wolly doodle all the day. [Stop.]
I thought I heard a chicken sneeze,
[Walk clockwise in circle.]
Sing Polly wolly doodle all the day. [Stop.]

Fare thee well, [Clap, clap.] fare thee well, [Clap, clap.]]
Fare thee well my fairy fay, [Clap, clap.]
For I'm going to Lou'siana for to see my Susyanna,
Sing Polly wolly doodle all the day. [Clap, clap.]

He sneezed so hard with the whooping cough,
[Walk counterclockwise in circle.]
Sing Polly wolly doodle all the day. [Stop.]
He sneezed his head and the tail right off,
[Walk clockwise in circle.]
Sing Polly wolly doodle all the day. [Stop.]

Fare thee well, [Clap, clap.] fare thee well, [Clap, clap.]
Fare thee well my fairy fay, [Clap, clap.]
For I'm going to Lou'siana for to see my Susyanna,
Sing Polly wolly doodle all the day. [Clap, clap.]

Oh, a grasshopper sittin' on a railroad track,
[Walk counterclockwise in circle.]
Sing Polly wolly doodle all the day. [Stop.]
A-pickin' his teeth with a carpet tack,
[Walk clockwise in circle.]
Sing Polly wolly doodle all the day. [Stop.]

Fare thee well, [Clap, clap.] fare thee well, [Clap, clap.]
Fare thee well my fairy fay, [Clap, clap.]
For I'm going to Lou'siana for to see my Susyanna.
Sing Polly wolly doodle all the day. [Clap, clap.]

Oh, I went to bed but it wasn't any use,
[Walk counterclockwise in circle.]
Sing Polly wolly doodle all the day. [Stop.]
My feet stuck out like a chicken roost,
[Walk clockwise in circle.]
Sing Polly wolly doodle all the day. [Stop.]

Fare thee well, [Clap, clap.] fare thee well, [Clap, clap.]
Fare thee well my fairy fay, [Clap, clap.]
For I'm going to Lou'siana for to see my Susyanna,
Sing Polly wolly doodle all the day. [Clap, clap.]

Polly Wolly Doodle All the Day

STAGING: The teacher and the narrators should all be seated on tall stools facing the audience.

| Teacher | Singer I | Singer II | Singer III |
| X | X | X | X |

TEACHER: Oh, I went down South for to see my Sal,

SINGERS: Sing Polly wolly doodle all the day.

TEACHER: My Sal, she is a spunky gal,

SINGERS: Sing Polly wolly doodle all the day.

TEACHER: Fare thee well, fare thee well, fare thee well my fairy fay, for I'm going to Lou'siana for to see my Susyanna,

SINGERS: Sing Polly wolly doodle all the day.

TEACHER: Oh, my Sal, she is a maiden fair,

SINGERS: Sing Polly wolly doodle all the day.

TEACHER: With curly eyes and laughing hair,

SINGERS: Sing Polly wolly doodle all the day,

TEACHER: Fare thee well, fare thee well, fare thee well my fairy fay, for I'm going to Lou'siana for to see my Susyanna,

SINGERS: Sing Polly wolly doodle all the day.

TEACHER: Behind the barn, down on my knees,

SINGERS: Sing Polly wolly doodle all the day.

TEACHER: I thought I heard a chicken sneeze,

From *Songs and Rhymes Readers Theatre for Beginning Readers* by Anthony D. Fredericks. Westport, CT: Teacher Ideas Press. Copyright © 2008.

SINGERS: Sing Polly wolly doodle all the day.

TEACHER: Fare thee well, fare thee well, fare thee well my fairy fay, for I'm going to Lou'siana for to see my Susyanna,

SINGERS: Sing Polly wolly doodle all the day.

TEACHER: He sneezed so hard with the whooping cough,

SINGERS: Sing Polly wolly doodle all the day.

TEACHER: He sneezed his head and the tail right off,

SINGERS: Sing Polly wolly doodle all the day.

TEACHER: Fare thee well, fare thee well, fare thee well my fairy fay, for I'm going to Lou'siana for to see my Susyanna,

SINGERS: Sing Polly wolly doodle all the day.

TEACHER: Oh, a grasshopper sittin' on a railroad track,

SINGERS: Sing Polly wolly doodle all the day.

TEACHER: A-pickin' his teeth with a carpet tack,

SINGERS: Sing Polly wolly doodle all the day.

TEACHER: Fare thee well, fare thee well, fare thee well my fairy fay, for I'm going to Lou'siana for to see my Susyanna,

SINGERS: Sing Polly wolly doodle all the day.

TEACHER: Oh, I went to bed but it wasn't any use,

SINGERS: Sing Polly wolly doodle all the day.

TEACHER: My feet stuck out like a chicken roost,

SINGERS: Sing Polly wolly doodle all the day.

TEACHER: Fare thee well, fare thee well, fare thee well my fairy fay, for I'm going to Lou'siana for to see my Susyanna,

EVERYBODY: Sing Polly wolly doodle all the day.

Hush, Little Baby

PRESENTATION SUGGESTIONS

This script has the song embedded inside another story. You may wish to introduce the song and the music to students in advance of a presentation so they are used to the rhyme and rhythm.

PROPS

Obtain a cradle or basinet to be placed in the center of the staging area. Place a doll or figurine in the cradle.

DELIVERY

The characters should be having a comfortable and easygoing conversation—similar to how they might converse on the playground.

MUSICAL VERSION

Log on to the following Web site for a musical version of the nursery rhyme: http://www. kinderplanet.com/hushlitt.htm.

The site plays the song over and over again. Plan to teach students the words to the song first. After they are comfortable with the words, encourage them to sing the song along with the music.

MOVEMENT/DANCE

Invite all the students to stand in a large circle. If possible, place a crib (with a baby doll in it) in the middle of the circle. Ask everyone to simulate the following movements as the rhyme is shared. (You may wish to read the rhyme out loud, or selected students may wish to read the rhyme to their classmates.)

Hush, little baby, don't say a word,
[Place a finger up to the lips to say "Shhhh."]
Poppa's gonna buy you a mockingbird.
[Cross hands over each other and link the thumbs. Flap the hands to simulate a flying bird.]
And if that mockingbird won't sing,
[Have students say, "La, la, la, la."]
Poppa's gonna buy you a diamond ring.
[Point to ring finger on left hand.]

And if that diamond ring turns to brass,
[Rub top of left hand with right hand.]
Poppa's gonna buy you a looking glass.
[Simulate looking through a telescope.]
And if that looking glass gets broke,
[Simulate dropping an item on the floor.]
Poppa's gonna buy you a billy goat.
[Make the sounds of a bleating goat.]

And if that billy goat won't pull,
[Simulate pulling a rope over the right shoulder.]
Poppa's gonna buy you a cart and bull.
[Place fists on sides of head with index fingers pointing upwards.]
And if that cart and bull turn over,
[Everyone turn their bodies sharply to the right.]
Poppa's gonna buy you a dog named Rover.
[Everybody make a single barking noise.]

And if that dog named Rover won't bark,
[Everybody open their mouths wide.]
Poppa's gonna buy you a horse and cart.
[Everybody stamp their feet.]
And if that horse and cart fall down,
[Everyone turn their bodies sharply to the left.]
You'll still be the sweetest little baby in town.
[Everybody take one step toward the cradle and look in.]

Hush, Little Baby

STAGING: The characters should all be standing. They may wish to have their scripts on individual music stands or held in their hands. The cradle or basinet should be placed in the center of the characters. A doll should be placed inside the cradle or basinet. There is no narrator for this script.

```
              Tom           Lucy          Anna          Terry
               X             X             X             X
      Scott          Jim           Francis       Luke
       X              X              X             X
                           (Cradle)
                              X
```

TOM: Hey, my mother had a new baby.

LUCY: I bet he's cute!

TOM: Well, he is really a she.

LUCY: I still bet that she's cute.

TOM: Yeah, I guess she is.

ANNA: What can she do?

TOM: Not much.

TERRY: Can she talk?

TOM: No.

SCOTT: Can she crawl?

TOM: No.

JIM: Can she use a computer?

TOM: NO!!!

FRANCIS: Well then, what can she do?

TOM: She can cry. She can burp. And she can sleep.

LUKE: Is that all?

From *Songs and Rhymes Readers Theatre for Beginning Readers* by Anthony D. Fredericks. Westport, CT: Teacher Ideas Press. Copyright © 2008.

TOM: Yeah, that's all!

LUCY: That's not much.

TOM: No, it's not. But she is only a few weeks old.

ANNA: Do you play with her?

TOM: Sometimes I do.

TERRY: What do you play?

TOM: I talk to her sometimes.

SCOTT: What else?

TOM: Sometimes I sing to her.

JIM: What do you sing?

TOM: I sing songs and stuff.

FRANCIS: What kind of songs?

TOM: Oh, just songs and stuff.

LUKE: Can you sing a song for us?

TOM: I can do better than that. I can teach you a song to sing.

LUCY: That sounds great.

ANNA: Yeah, I can hardly wait.

TERRY: So, how does this song go?

SCOTT: Is it an easy song?

JIM: Is it a hard song?

FRANCIS: Is it an old song?

LUKE: Is it a fun song?

TOM: It's a real easy song. Just follow the words in your script. Are you ready?

SCOTT: Let's go. Tom, you can start.

TOM: Hush, little baby,

LUCY: Don't say a word,

ANNA: Poppa's gonna buy you

TERRY: A mockingbird.

SCOTT: And if that mockingbird

JIM: Won't sing,

FRANCIS: Poppa's gonna buy you

LUKE: A diamond ring.

TOM: And if that diamond ring

LUCY: Turns to brass,

ANNA: Poppa's gonna buy you

TERRY: A looking glass.

SCOTT: And if that looking glass

JIM: Gets broke,

FRANCIS: Poppa's gonna buy you

LUKE: A billy goat.

TOM: And if that billy goat

LUCY: Won't pull,

ANNA: Poppa's gonna buy you

TERRY: A cart and bull.

SCOTT: And if that cart and bull

JIM: Turn over,

FRANCIS: Poppa's gonna buy you

LUKE: A dog named Rover.

TOM: And if that dog named Rover

LUCY: Won't bark,

ANNA: Poppa's gonna buy you

TERRY: A horse and cart.

SCOTT: And if that horse and cart

JIM: Fall down,

FRANCIS: You'll still be the sweetest

LUKE: Little baby in town.

ALL: THE END!

If You're Happy and You Know It

PRESENTATION SUGGESTIONS

Many students will be familiar with this song. However, it is suggested that you play the song for all students several times in advance of the readers theatre presentation so that everyone is familiar with the pace and cadence of the music (and the accompanying lyrics).

PROPS

There are no props for this presentation.

DELIVERY

The characters should all be animated and lively. The narrator may talk in a serious and businesslike tone of voice. The characters should be encouraged to prance around the staging area, pointing at the audience, and laughing whenever appropriate. This is a lively song that will have everyone engaged and active.

MUSICAL VERSION

Log on to the following Web site for an upbeat and engaging version of this song: http://www.niehs.nih.gov/kids/lyrics/happyand.htm.

As noted above, consider playing this song several times before presenting the script.

MOVEMENT/DANCE

This script is filled with lots of movement and singing parts for both the players and the audience. After students are comfortable with the song (and the accompanying movements), they may wish to sing it at various times during the school day. I always liked to "drop in" a question or two after recess, before silent reading, or just as students were lining up for afternoon buses. ("If you're happy and you know it, clap your hands.")

Invite youngsters to think up some other movements or actions for this song. Here are a few my students created:

"If you're happy and you know it,

- ❖ . . . blink your eyes."

- ❖ . . . wave your arms."

- ❖ . . . shake your hips."

- ❖ . . . tickle your friend."

- ❖ . . . eat a worm." [Simulated with gummy worms.]

- ❖ . . . make a face."

- ❖ . . . read a book."

If You're Happy and You Know It

STAGING: The characters should all be standing. They should be encouraged to interact with the audience as much as possible (pointing, walking toward the audience, etc.). The narrator can also be standing or placed at a lectern or music stand.

```
                                               Narrator
                                                  X
            Cassie            Lamanda
              X                  X
       Jerrill                         Juan
          X                             X
```

NARRATOR: Is everybody happy?

JERRILL: I'm happy!

CASSIE: I'm happy, too.

LAMANDA: I'm very, very happy.

JUAN: It looks like everybody here is happy. What about them [points to audience]?

NARRATOR: Well, folks, are you all happy?

AUDIENCE: YES!

NARRATOR: Well, it looks like everybody here is happy.

JERRILL: Hey, I have a question. How do we know when people are happy?

LAMANDA: Well, if they are smiling, then they must be happy.

CASSIE: Yeah, that's right—when people smile, then they are happy.

JERRILL: Can someone be happy and not smile?

JUAN: I guess so.

From *Songs and Rhymes Readers Theatre for Beginning Readers* by Anthony D. Fredericks. Westport, CT: Teacher Ideas Press. Copyright © 2008.

LAMANDA: How would that person show it?

JERRILL: What do you mean?

LAMANDA: Can someone be happy and not be smiling?

CASSIE: I guess he could. But how would you know?

JUAN: I guess if she was singing, then she would be happy.

LAMANDA: That sounds right. If he was dancing, then he would be happy.

JERRILL: That sounds right. How else could someone be happy?

CASSIE: Maybe if she was cheering or shouting, then she would be happy.

JUAN: That sounds right.

LAMANDA: Well, maybe we should ask the audience [points to audience].

NARRATOR: OK, audience, are you ready to show us how you are happy?

AUDIENCE: YES! YES! YES!

NARRATOR: OK, let's go!

[Consider playing the music for the remainder of this script.]

CASSIE: If you're happy and you know it, clap your hands

AUDIENCE: [clap, clap]

LAMANDA: If you're happy and you know it, clap your hands

AUDIENCE: [clap, clap]

JERRILL: If you're happy and you know it, then your face will surely show it.

JUAN: If you're happy and you know it, clap your hands.

AUDIENCE: [clap, clap]

CASSIE: If you're happy and you know it, stomp your feet

AUDIENCE: [stomp, stomp]

LAMANDA: If you're happy and you know it, stomp your feet

AUDIENCE: [stomp, stomp]

JERRILL: If you're happy and you know it, then your face will surely show it.

JUAN: If you're happy and you know it, stomp your feet.

AUDIENCE: [stomp, stomp]

CASSIE: If you're happy and you know it, shout "Hurray!"

AUDIENCE: HOO-RAY!

LAMANDA: If you're happy and you know it, shout "Hurray!"

AUDIENCE: HOO-RAY!

JERRILL: If you're happy and you know it, then your face will surely show it.

JUAN: If you're happy and you know it, shout "Hurray!"

AUDIENCE: HOO-RAY!

CASSIE: If you're happy and you know it, do all three.

AUDIENCE: [clap-clap, stomp-stomp] HOO-RAY!

LAMANDA: If you're happy and you know it, do all three.

AUDIENCE: [clap-clap, stomp-stomp] HOO-RAY!

JERRILL: If you're happy and you know it, then your face will surely show it.

JUAN: If you're happy and you know it, do all three.

AUDIENCE: [clap-clap, stomp-stomp] HOO-RAY!

I'm a Little Teapot

PRESENTATION SUGGESTIONS

This script uses the "teapot song" embedded in another story. You may wish to introduce the song to students in advance of the readers theatre presentation or, for the first time, as it is included here within the script.

PROPS

You may wish to show students what an actual teapot (ceramic or metal) looks like (one of your own or one borrowed from a friend). Afterward you can place the teapot on a small table in the middle of the staging area.

DELIVERY

The characters should all be having a comfortable and friendly conversation—similar to what they would have on the playground or during recess.

MUSICAL VERSION

Log on to the following Web site for a quick-paced and upbeat version of this song: www. kinderplanet.com/music.htm.

Click on "I'm a Little Teapot." This Web site repeats the song over and over. Share the lyrics (below) with students and invite them to sing along to the musical accompaniment.

MOVEMENT/DANCE

One individual stands in front of the other students (or in the middle of a circle of students). He or she takes on the role of the "teapot" as the song is read or sung by the teacher or all the other students in the class. One or two other students may wish to take on the role of the "teapot."

I'm a little teapot, [Points to self.]
short and stout.
Here is my handle, [Left hand on hip.]
Here is my spout.
[Right arm out with elbow and wrist bent.]
When I get all steamed up, [Excited look on face.]
Hear me shout. [Says loudly.]
Just tip me over and pour me out.
[Bend at waist toward right arm as if pouring tea out of the spout.]

I'm a clever teapot, [Points to self.]
Yes it's true. [Nod head.]
Here, let me show you what I do. [Right hand on hip.]
I can change my handle to my spout.
[Left arm out with elbow and wrist bent.]
Just tip me over and pour me out.
[Bend at waist toward left arm as if pouring tea out of the spout.]

I'm a Little Teapot

STAGING: The characters can be seated on stools or chairs. They may also be standing or placed at individual lecterns. The Teapot should be standing in the middle of the other characters—next to a small table or desk on which is placed an actual teapot.

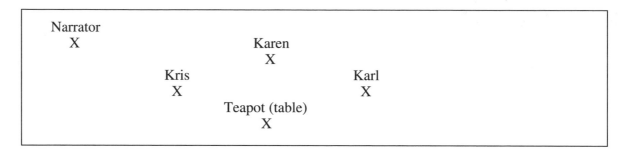

Narrator		
X		
	Karen	
	X	
Kris		Karl
X		X
	Teapot (table)	
	X	

NARRATOR:	Once upon a time there was a teapot.
TEAPOT:	That's me!
NARRATOR:	Now this teapot was short and stout.
TEAPOT:	Hey, wait a minute! What does that mean?
KRIS:	I think it means that you are fat!
TEAPOT:	Hey, that's not nice!
KAREN:	You're right. It isn't nice.
KARL:	But, you must remember—this story is very old.
KRIS:	Is it as old as our teacher?
KARL:	Oh, not THAT old. But it's still very old.
KAREN:	OK, so it's an old story.
KRIS:	Yeah, and sometime people in the old days liked to make up stories.
KARL:	That's right. Just like we do today.
KAREN:	And sometimes they liked to use words that rhymed.
KARL:	Right. Just like we do today.

From *Songs and Rhymes Readers Theatre for Beginning Readers* by Anthony D. Fredericks. Westport, CT: Teacher Ideas Press. Copyright © 2008.

KRIS: Whoever wrote this story wanted to use a word. The author wanted to use a word that would rhyme with other words.

KAREN: That's right. A word like *stout*?

KARL: Yes, "stout" can rhyme with lots of words.

KRIS: Let's see how many we know.

KAREN: There's *doubt* and *pout*.

KARL: And *scout, shout,* and *spout*.

KRIS: And, don't forget *sprout, trout,* and *about*.

KARL: And also just plain *out*.

KAREN: Wow, lots of words.

TEAPOT: Hey, that's all fine. But what about my story?

NARRATOR: Yeah, guys, what about the teapot's story?

KAREN: You're right. We almost forgot.

KARL: So, little teapot short and stout. Are you ready with your story?

TEAPOT: I'm ready. Let's go!

NARRATOR: OK, here we go!

TEAPOT: I'm a little teapot,
Short and stout.
Here is my handle,
Here is my spout.
When I get all steamed up,
Hear me shout.
Just tip me over,
And pour me out.

ALL: YEAH!

KRIS: Hey, I have an idea.

KAREN: What's that?

KRIS: Why don't we help out?

KARL: What do you mean?

KRIS: Well, isn't there another part to the song?

KAREN: Yes.

KRIS: So, we could help our friend here (points to Teapot) . . . .

KARL: I know, by saying that part ourselves.

KRIS: Right. Are you guys ready?

ALL: YES!!

KRIS: OK, Teapot, start us off.

TEAPOT: I'm a little teapot,
Short and stout.
Here is my handle,
Here is my spout.
When I get all steamed up,
Hear me shout.
Just tip me over,
And pour me out.

[The following part of the script can be presented in a singsong cadence.]

KRIS: I'm a clever teapot,

KAREN: Yes, it's true

KARL: Here, let me show you

KRIS: What I do.

KAREN: I can change my handle

KARL: To my spout.

KRIS: Just tip me over,

KAREN: And . . .

KARL: . . . pour . . .

KRIS: . . . me . . .

KAREN: . . . out!

NARRATOR: THE END!

It's Raining, It's Pouring

PRESENTATION SUGGESTIONS

This script uses the "Raining, Pouring" song embedded in another story. Consider introducing the song to students in advance of the presentation and then invite them to listen for the lyrics in the script as it is being presented.

PROPS

The only prop necessary will be a blanket or rug (see "Staging") in the middle of the staging area.

DELIVERY

The characters should all be having a light conversation—similar to what they might do if they were on the playground or at recess.

MUSICAL VERSION

Log on to the following Web site for a musical rendition of this well-known song: http://www. niehs.nih.gov/kids/lyrics/itsraining.htm.

The music will play over and over again. Share the lyrics from the Web page or those below with your students and invite them to sing along with the musical accompaniment.

47

MOVEMENT/DANCE

I like to have students stand in a large circle. As each line of the song is sung, the students can perform selected actions with their hands and other body parts.

It's raining, it's pouring,
[Students all raise their arms in the air and wiggle their fingers.]
The old man is snoring.
[Students clasp their hands together and put them on one side of their heads as though they are sleeping—snoring sounds are optional.]
He went to bed,
[Students reach down to the floor and pull up an imaginary blanket over their heads.]
And bumped his head,
[Students tap the front of their foreheads lightly with their fists.]
And couldn't get up in the morning.
[Students raise their arms again and let out some loud yawns.]

[Repeat.]

It's Raining, It's Pouring

STAGING: The characters should all be standing. Each one can be standing at a lectern or simply holding her or his script. The "old man" can be lying on a blanket on the floor in the middle of the staging area. If possible, put a blanket on a short table and invite the "old man" to lie on the table. The "old man" should be softly snoring throughout this presentation.

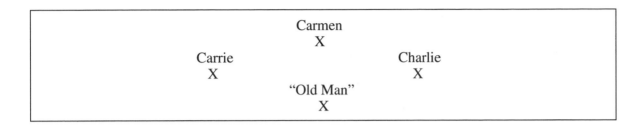

CARRIE: Hey, look! [points to "Old Man"]

CARMEN: What?

CHARLIE: It looks like an old man.

CARRIE: You're right. It is an old man.

CARMEN: What is he doing here?

CHARLIE: I don't know.

CARRIE: It looks like he's sleeping.

CARMEN: Why is he sleeping?

CHARLIE: Maybe he's sleepy.

CARRIE: Maybe he didn't want to go to recess.

CARMEN: Old men don't go to recess.

CHARLIE: Maybe he DID go to recess, but got real tired.

CARRIE: He sure can snore.

CARMEN: Yeah, he sure can.

CHARLIE: He sounds like my grandmother.

From *Songs and Rhymes Readers Theatre for Beginning Readers* by Anthony D. Fredericks. Westport, CT: Teacher Ideas Press. Copyright © 2008.

CARRIE: Does your grandmother snore?

CHARLIE: You bet she does. She snores so loud it keeps everybody awake.

CARMEN: Wow, she's a loud snorer.

CARRIE: Just like our friend. [points to "Old Man"]

CHARLIE: Why does he snore all the time?

CARMEN: Maybe he swallowed a fly.

CARRIE: Or maybe he ate an elephant.

CHARLIE: AN ELEPHANT! How could he swallow an elephant?

CARRIE: My dad eats stuff all the time.

CARMEN: Does your dad eat elephants?

CARRIE: No. But one time he said he was so hungry that he could eat a horse.

CHARLIE: So, your father eats horses?

CARRIE: I don't think so, but he sure does eat a lot!

CARMEN: Maybe our friend here [points to "Old Man"] bumped his head.

CHARLIE: Why?

CARMEN: Well, I bumped my head once.

CARRIE: Did it make you snore?

CARMEN: No, I don't think so. But, it sure did hurt.

CHARLIE: Maybe old people snore when they hit their heads.

CARRIE: Maybe they do. Old people do funny things.

CARMEN: Yeah, like Charlie's grandmother.

CHARLIE: You mean my snoring grandmother!

CARRIE: Well, what do we do now?

CARMEN: Well, maybe we can sing a song.

CHARLIE: I like to sing!

CARRIE: So do I.

CARMEN: Then, let's sing a song about our snoring friend here.

CHARLIE: OK!

CARRIE: OK!

CARMEN: Here we go. It's raining,

CHARLIE: It's pouring,

CARRIE: The old man is snoring.

CARMEN: He went to bed,

CHARLIE: And bumped his head,

CARRIE: And couldn't get up in the morning.

CARMEN: If he couldn't get up in the morning then he couldn't go to recess.

CHARLIE: Poor old man.

CARRIE: Poor old man

ALL: Bye, bye, old man.

[They all exit the staging area].

On Top of Spaghetti

PRESENTATION SUGGESTIONS

This script uses the lyrics from the song "On Top of Spaghetti" as part of the presentation. Plan to play the music in the second part of the presentation so that the characters can sing their lines along with the music. You may wish to print the lyrics on a sheet of lined chart pack paper so that the audience can sing along with the players.

PROPS

You may wish to place several cans of spaghetti on a table in the middle of the staging area. Or you may want to construct a very large papier mâché meatball and place it in the center of the staging area.

DELIVERY

Students should all converse as if they were on the playground or in the classroom. The tone should be friendly and conversational. The narrator should also have a friendly tone of voice.

MUSICAL VERSION

Log on to the following Web site for a slow-paced version of this popular summer camp song: http://www.niehs.nih.gov/kids/lyrics/ontopofspag.htm.

Students will be able to keep up with the tempo of this song as they say their lines (lyrics). After sufficient practice, invite the audience to sing along with the players.

MOVEMENT/DANCE

Invite the entire class to participate in the following rendition of the song. Gather all the students into a very large circle. All students should be facing the interior of the circle.

On top of spaghetti,
[Point to center of circle.]
All covered with cheese,
[Pretend to shake parmesan cheese.]
I lost my poor meatball,
[Hunch shoulders and shake head.]
When somebody sneezed.
[Simulate sneezing; cover mouth with hand.]

It rolled off the table,
[Roll both hands over and over.]
And onto the floor,
[Point to the floor.]
And then my poor meatball
[Hands together in round shape.]
Rolled out of the door.
[Roll both hands over and over.]

It rolled down the garden,
[Roll both hands over and over.]
And under a bush,
[Bend over and point to the left.]
And then my poor meatball
[Hands together in round shape.]
Was nothing but mush!
[Wiggle fingers all around.]

The mush was as tasty,
[Simulate eating with fork.]
As tasty could be. [Lick lips.]
And then the next summer,
[Wipe brow with one hand.]
It grew into a tree.
[Hands together and move from floor upwards.]

The tree was all covered,
[Move hands all around.]
All covered with moss, [Hold nose.]
And on it grew meatballs,
[Hands together in round shape.]
All covered with sauce.
[Simulate pouring a jar of sauce.]

So if you have spaghetti,
[Point to center of circle.]
All covered with cheese,
[Pretend to shake parmesan cheese.]
Hold onto your meatball,
[Hold hands together.]
'Cause someone might sneeze.
[Simulate sneezing; cover mouth with hand.]

On Top of Spaghetti

STAGING: The characters can all be seated on chairs or stools. The narrator can be off to the side standing at a lectern or music stand.

```
                                                    Narrator
                                                       X
        Devin                    William
          X                         X
                  Melanie                      Brad
                     X                          X
```

NARRATOR: Once upon a time there were four students. They all worked very hard. They learned how to read. They learned how to add and subtract. They learned all about plants and animals. They were very smart students. But all of that hard work made all of them very hungry. They couldn't wait for lunch. Let's listen in.

MELANIE: Boy, am I hungry!

DEVIN: Yeah, I'm hungry, too!

WILLIAM: You know, all of this learning makes me hungry!

BRAD: Me, too.

MELANIE: I wonder when lunch will be.

DEVIN: I don't know if I can wait.

BRAD: I hope it comes soon. I'm starving.

WILLIAM: So am I.

DEVIN: Does anybody know what we're having?

BRAD: I wasn't listening to the announcements.

MELANIE: Neither was I.

WILLIAM: I hope it's something good.

MELANIE: Me, too.

WILLIAM: Didn't our teacher [points to teacher] say we're having spaghetti?

DEVIN: Spaghetti! UMMMMM! I love spaghetti.

MELANIE: I like spaghetti better than hamburgers.

WILLIAM: I like spaghetti better than peanut butter sandwiches.

BRAD: I think I love spaghetti better than anything.

WILLIAM: You mean, better than ice cream?

BRAD: Welllllll, maybe not as much as ice cream.

WILLIAM: How about spaghetti with ice cream on top?

MELANIE: Ohhhhh, gross!

DEVIN: Yeah, that's really gross.

BRAD: Hey, I have an idea.

MELANIE: What's that?

BRAD: Why don't we make up a song about spaghetti?

DEVIN: Hey, that sounds great! I mean, we're really smart. Making a song should be fun.

MELANIE: So, what do we do?

BRAD: Well, let's think of something funny. A funny song about spaghetti would be fun.

ALL: OK.

NARRATOR: And so our very smart students began to write. They wrote a song about spaghetti. They wrote a funny song about spaghetti. They worked really hard. They would like to sing their song for you. So listen carefully. Their song is called "On Top of Spaghetti." Are you ready? Here goes.

MELANIE: On top of spaghetti,

DEVIN: All covered with cheese,

WILLIAM: I lost my poor meatball,

BRAD: When somebody sneezed.

MELANIE: It rolled off the table,

DEVIN: And onto the floor,

WILLIAM: And then my poor meatball

BRAD: Rolled out of the door.

MELANIE: It rolled down the garden,

DEVIN: And under a bush,

WILLIAM: And then my poor meatball

BRAD: Was nothing but mush!

MELANIE: The mush was as tasty,

DEVIN: As tasty could be,

WILLIAM: And then the next summer,

BRAD: It grew into a tree.

MELANIE: The tree was all covered,

DEVIN: All covered with moss,

WILLIAM: And on it grew meatballs,

BRAD: All covered with sauce.

MELANIE: So if you have spaghetti,

DEVIN: All covered with cheese,

WILLIAM: Hold onto your meatball,

BRAD: 'Cause someone might sneeze.

[Repeat the song while playing the accompanying music.]

MELANIE: On top of spaghetti,

DEVIN: All covered with cheese,

WILLIAM: I lost my poor meatball,

BRAD: When somebody sneezed.

MELANIE: It rolled off the table,

DEVIN: And onto the floor,

WILLIAM: And then my poor meatball

BRAD: Rolled out of the door.

MELANIE: It rolled down the garden,

DEVIN: And under a bush,

WILLIAM: And then my poor meatball

BRAD: Was nothing but mush!

MELANIE: The mush was as tasty,

DEVIN: As tasty could be,

WILLIAM: And then the next summer,

BRAD: It grew into a tree.

MELANIE: The tree was all covered,

DEVIN: All covered with moss,

WILLIAM: And on it grew meatballs,

BRAD: All covered with sauce.

MELANIE: So if you have spaghetti,

DEVIN: All covered with cheese,

WILLIAM: Hold onto your meatball,

BRAD: 'Cause someone might sneeze.

NARRATOR: And that's the end of our story. Now, let's go have some lunch!

Shoo Fly

PRESENTATION SUGGESTIONS

This script should be used as an introduction to the song "Shoo Fly." Invite selected students to practice the script (first) and the lyrics of the song (second). When sufficiently practiced, invite them to share the script and their rendition of the song. Invite the players to teach the song to the other members of the class in preparation for a whole class sing-along.

PROPS

You may wish to post a large photograph of a fly (or flies) on the wall behind the players.

DELIVERY

The students should speak in a normal tone of voice—similar to what they would use in the classroom or on the playground. The narrator should talk in a more formal way.

MUSICAL VERSION

Log on to the following Web site for an upbeat version of the song. The music allows students to sing the song through two complete times: http://www.niehs.nih.gov/kids/lyrics/shoofly.htm.

MOVEMENT/DANCE

After students have learned the music and lyrics of the song, invite them to add the following movements. When students have used these movements in one or two sing-alongs, invite them to create alternate movements for other renditions of the song.

Shoo, fly, don't bother me, [Swat the air.]
Shoo, fly, don't bother me, [Swat the air.]
Shoo, fly, don't bother me, [Swat the air.]
For I belong to somebody.
[Point to person nearby.]

I feel, I feel,
[Cross arms and sway to and fro.]
I feel like a morning star. [Point upwards.]
I feel, I feel,
[Cross arms and sway to and fro.]
I feel like a morning star. [Point upwards.]

[Repeat.]

Shoo Fly

STAGING: The narrator sits on a stool in front of the characters. The characters should be standing in a loose group.

```
      Lorna
        X          Lisa
                     X
           Larry
             X              Logan
                              X           Narrator
                                             X
```

NARRATOR: Welcome to ABC Elementary School. We are visiting Miss Smith's classroom. The students are talking. Let's listen.

LORNA: Boy, it sure is hot today.

LISA: You bet it is.

LARRY: I think this is the hottest day ever.

LOGAN: I can't believe how hot it is!

LORNA: You know what I don't like?

LISA: What's that?

LORNA: I don't like all the flies.

LARRY: Yeah, me too.

LOGAN: Yeah, me too too!

LORNA: Flies are dirty.

LISA: And flies buzz all the time.

LARRY: And flies bother me.

LOGAN: And they always land on me.

LORNA: I just wish those darn flies would go away.

From *Songs and Rhymes Readers Theatre for Beginning Readers* by Anthony D. Fredericks. Westport, CT: Teacher Ideas Press. Copyright © 2008.

LISA: Yeah, they sure are pests.

LARRY: How could we make them go away?

LOGAN: Maybe we could swat them.

LORNA: Swat them, what's that?

LOGAN: That's when you take a fly swatter and hit them hard.

LORNA: Then what happens?

LOGAN: You kill the fly.

LISA: But, aren't there still more flies?

LOGAN: Yeah, swatting only works for one fly at a time.

LARRY: That's not very good.

LISA: No, it isn't.

LORNA: What else could we do?

LISA: You could use fly spray.

LORNA: Yeah, but that stuff stinks.

LISA: Yes, it does. But it makes the flies stay away.

LORNA: I don't like that stuff.

LARRY: I think it could be dangerous.

LOGAN: You're probably right.

LISA: Have you heard about fly strips?

LARRY: I've heard about those.

LISA: Yeah, you hang them up. Then the flies come and get stuck on them. Pretty soon they're covered with flies.

LORNA: That's sounds pretty gross.

LARRY: It is.

NARRATOR: The students keep talking. Then someone gets an idea. It's a crazy idea, but it might work.

LORNA: Hey, I have an idea.

LISA: What's that?

LORNA: Why don't we sing the flies away?

LARRY: What?

LORNA: Why don't we sing the flies away?

LOGAN: What are you talking about?

LORNA: If we sing really loud, maybe the flies will stay away.

LISA: Hey, maybe you're right.

LORNA: I think I am. Maybe flies don't like music.

LARRY: We like music.

LOGAN: But maybe flies don't.

LORNA: So, what do you say? Should we sing?

LISA: Yeah, let's try it.

LARRY: It would be safer than fly strips.

LOGAN: And it wouldn't smell funny.

LORNA: OK, let's try it out!

NARRATOR: So the students wrote a song. They sang the song. And, guess what? That's right. The flies stayed away. So, now it's your turn [points to audience] to sing the song. Ready? Here goes.

[Play the music and invite the characters to sing the song "Shoo Fly" first. Then invite the rest of the class to participate in a group singing of the song.]

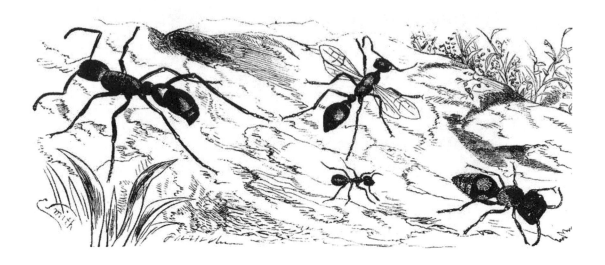

The Ants Go Marching

PRESENTATION SUGGESTIONS

Print the song on large sheets of newsprint or on chart paper. Teach the song to the students while pointing to the words as you sing them together. Plan some time for students to practice the movements (see "Staging") so that they are comfortable with the lyrics and the movements together.

PROPS

No props are necessary for this script.

DELIVERY

Since this entire readers theatre script is the singing of the song "The Ants Go Marching," you may wish to have students practice their lines as though they were singing a song.

MUSICAL VERSION

You may wish to log on to the following Web site so that students can hear the music that typically accompanies the lyrics of the song: http://www.niehs.nih.gov/kids/lyrics/antsgo.htm.

It is not necessary to play the music as students are saying or performing their various parts throughout this song. In fact, I have found it advantageous to eliminate the accompanying music so that students are not hampered by the pace of the music in accomplishing the various physical movements (large groups of students moving to the front of the room prior to verses near the end of the song) necessary throughout the script.

MOVEMENT/DANCE

There is sufficient movement for all students throughout this script. Designated students (and groups of students) will need to quickly move to the front of the class and then perform a marching action at appropriate points in the production. Practicing these movements in advance of the presentation is strongly suggested.

The Ants Go Marching

STAGING: This script is designed to allow for maximum participation by all members of the class. All students should be standing. As each character part comes up, the designated student(s) come to the front of the room, turn around to face the rest of the class, say their lines, and perform their parts. For example, for "The ants go marching one by one," one student stands in front of the others and says his or her lines while marching in place during the singing of that verse. For "The ants go marching two by two," two students get up, speak, and "march" in front of the class as that verse is being sung. This continues throughout the song until the very end, when all the students in the class jump up and shout, "THE END."

```
                        (staging area)


                    X X X X X X X X
                  X X X X X X X X  X
                    X X X X X X X
                  X X X X X X X X X
                        (class)
```

ONE STUDENT: The ants go marching one by one, [in front of class]

CLASS: Hurrah, hurrah!

ONE STUDENT: The ants go marching one by one,

CLASS: Hurrah, hurrah!

ONE STUDENT: The ants go marching one by one.
The little one stops to suck his thumb.
And they all go marching

CLASS: Down to the ground
To get out of the rain.
BOOM! BOOM! BOOM!

TWO STUDENTS: The ants go marching two by two, [in front of class]

CLASS: Hurrah, hurrah!

TWO STUDENTS: The ants go marching two by two,

CLASS: Hurrah, hurrah!

TWO STUDENTS: The ants go marching two by two.
The little one stops to tie his shoe.
And they all go marching

CLASS: Down to the ground
To get out of the rain.
BOOM! BOOM! BOOM!

THREE STUDENTS: The ants go marching three by three, [in front of class]

CLASS: Hurrah, hurrah!

THREE STUDENTS: The ants go marching three by three,

CLASS: Hurrah, hurrah!

THREE STUDENTS: The ants go marching three by three.
The little one stops to climb a tree.
And they all go marching,

CLASS: Down to the ground
To get out of the rain.
BOOM! BOOM! BOOM!

FOUR STUDENTS: The ants go marching four by four, [in front of class]

CLASS: Hurrah, hurrah!

FOUR STUDENTS: The ants go marching four by four,

CLASS: Hurrah, hurrah!

FOUR STUDENTS: The ants go marching four by four.
The little one stops to shut the door.
And they all go marching,

CLASS: Down to the ground
To get out of the rain.
BOOM! BOOM! BOOM!

FIVE STUDENTS: The ants go marching five by five, [in front of class]

CLASS: Hurrah, hurrah!

FIVE STUDENTS: The ants go marching five by five,

CLASS: Hurrah, hurrah!

FIVE STUDENTS: The ants go marching five by five.
The little one stops to take a dive.
And they all go marching,

CLASS: Down to the ground
To get out of the rain.
BOOM! BOOM! BOOM!

SIX STUDENTS: The ants go marching six by six, [in front of class]

CLASS: Hurrah, hurrah!

SIX STUDENTS: The ants go marching six by six,

CLASS: Hurrah, hurrah!

SIX STUDENTS: The ants go marching six by six.
The little one stops to pick up sticks.
And they all go marching,

CLASS: Down to the ground
To get out of the rain.
BOOM! BOOM! BOOM!

SEVEN STUDENTS: The ants go marching seven by seven, [in front of class]

CLASS: Hurrah, hurrah!

SEVEN STUDENTS: The ants go marching seven by seven,

CLASS: Hurrah, hurrah!

SEVEN STUDENTS: The ants go marching seven by seven.
The little one stops to pray to heaven.
And they all go marching,

CLASS: Down to the ground
To get out of the rain.
BOOM! BOOM! BOOM!

EIGHT STUDENTS: The ants go marching eight by eight, [in front of class]

CLASS: Hurrah, hurrah!

EIGHT STUDENTS: The ants go marching eight by eight,

CLASS: Hurrah, hurrah!

EIGHT STUDENTS: The ants go marching eight by eight.
The little one stops to shut the gate.
And they all go marching,

CLASS: Down to the ground
To get out of the rain.
BOOM! BOOM! BOOM!

NINE STUDENTS: The ants go marching nine by nine, [in front of class]

CLASS: Hurrah, hurrah!

NINE STUDENTS: The ants go marching nine by nine,

CLASS: Hurrah, hurrah!

NINE STUDENTS: The ants go marching nine by nine.
The little one stops to check the time.
And they all go marching,

CLASS: Down to the ground
To get out of the rain.
BOOM! BOOM! BOOM!

TEN STUDENTS: The ants go marching ten by ten, [in front of class]

CLASS: Hurrah, hurrah!

TEN STUDENTS: The ants go marching ten by ten,

CLASS: Hurrah, hurrah!

TEN STUDENTS: The ants go marching ten by ten.
The little one stops to say

CLASS: "THE END"

Mulberry Bush

PRESENTATION SUGGESTIONS

This script uses the song embedded in another story. You may wish to introduce the song to students in advance of the presentation or as part of a follow-up activity after the presentation.

PROPS

If possible, place a small potted plant or bush in the middle of the staging area. You may wish to hang a sign on the plant indicating that it is a "Mulberry Bush."

DELIVERY

If the characters are familiar with the song, they may wish to "sing" the lyrics to the song as they appear in this script. You may wish to play the music in the background as the script is being delivered.

MUSICAL VERSION

Log on to the following Web site for a musical rendition of this song: http://www.niehs. nih.gov/kids/lyrics/mulberry.htm.

This version is quick-paced and rapid. You may wish to have students listen to the music several times so that they are accustomed to the tempo of this song.

MOVEMENT/DANCE

Arrange all the students in a large circle. Ask students to face into the circle. Play the song for students and invite them to sing along. For each of the stanzas, invite them to perform the designated movements.

Here we go round the mulberry bush,
[Dance around in a clockwise rotation holding hands.]
The mulberry bush, the mulberry bush.
Here we go round the mulberry bush,
So early in the morning.

This is the way we wash our clothes,
[Simulate scrubbing action with both hands.]
Wash our clothes, wash our clothes.
This is the way we wash our clothes,
So early Monday morning

This is the way we iron our clothes,
[Simulate ironing action.]
Iron our clothes, iron our clothes.
This is the way we iron our clothes,
So early Tuesday morning.

This is the way we mend our clothes,
[Simulate sewing action.]
Mend our clothes, mend our clothes.
This is the way we mend our clothes,
So early Wednesday morning.

This is the way we sweep the floor,
[Simulate sweeping motion.]
Sweep the floor, sweep the floor.
This is the way we sweep the floor,
So early Thursday morning.

This is the way we scrub the floor,
[Simulate scrubbing motion.]
Scrub the floor, scrub the floor.
This is the way we scrub the floor,
So early Friday morning.

This is the way we bake our bread,
[Simulate opening over door and putting something in.]
Bake our bread, bake our bread.
This is the way we bake our bread,
So early Saturday morning.

This is the way we go to church,
[Dance around in a clockwise rotation holding hands.]
Go to church, go to church.
This is the way we go to church,
So early Sunday morning.

Mulberry Bush

STAGING: The narrator sits off to the side on a tall stool or chair. The other characters can be standing or sitting on chairs.

	Patty	Betty	Tommy			
Narrator	X	X	X			
X						
				Chorus		
				X	X	X
				X	X	

NARRATOR: Hey, is everybody ready for some fun?

PATTY: Yes!

BETTY: You bet we are!

TOMMY: Yeah, let's have some fun

NARRATOR: All right. This story is about a mulberry bush.

PATTY: A mulberry bush . . . what's that?

NARRATOR: Well, a mulberry bush has mulberries.

BETTY: Hey, what are mulberries?

NARRATOR: Well, mulberries are tiny fruits. They look like blackberries.

TOMMY: Do they taste the same?

NARRATOR: No, they have their own taste.

PATTY: Where do they grow?

NARRATOR: They grow up and down the east coast.

BETTY: How long does a mulberry bush live?

NARRATOR: Some bear fruit for hundreds of years.

PATTY: Wow, that's a long time. What do they taste like?

From *Songs and Rhymes Readers Theatre for Beginning Readers* by Anthony D. Fredericks. Westport, CT: Teacher Ideas Press. Copyright © 2008.

NARRATOR: They taste sweet. Some people say they taste like raspberries.

TOMMY: All this talk about mulberries is making me hungry!

BETTY: Me too.

PATTY: And those people, too. [points to Chorus]

NARRATOR: Well, why don't we do our script?

TOMMY: That sounds great. Let's go!

PATTY: Here we go round the mulberry bush,

CHORUS: The mulberry bush, the mulberry bush.

BETTY: Here we go round the mulberry bush,

CHORUS: So early in the morning.

TOMMY: This is the way we wash our clothes,

CHORUS: Wash our clothes, wash our clothes.

PATTY: This is the way we wash our clothes,

CHORUS: So early Monday morning.

BETTY: This is the way we iron our clothes,

CHORUS: Iron our clothes, iron our clothes.

TOMMY: This is the way we iron our clothes,

CHORUS: So early Tuesday morning.

PATTY: This is the way we mend our clothes,

CHORUS: Mend our clothes, mend our clothes.

BETTY: This is the way we mend our clothes,

CHORUS: So early Wednesday morning.

TOMMY: This is the way we sweep the floor,

CHORUS: Sweep the floor, sweep the floor.

PATTY: This is the way we sweep the floor,

CHORUS: So early Thursday morning.

BETTY: This is the way we scrub the floor,

CHORUS: Scrub the floor, scrub the floor.

TOMMY: This is the way we scrub the floor,

CHORUS: So early Friday morning.

PATTY: This is the way we bake our bread,

CHORUS: Bake our bread, bake our bread.

BETTY: This is the way we bake our bread,

CHORUS: So early Saturday morning.

TOMMY: This is the way we go to church,

CHORUS: Go to church, go to church.

PATTY: This is the way we go to church,

CHORUS: So early Sunday morning.

NARRATOR: And that, ladies and gentlemen, is the story of the mulberry bush.

BETTY: Yes, the delicious mulberry bush.

TOMMY: The very, very delicious mulberry bush.

NARRATOR: Hey, everybody, I'm hungry. Let's go eat!

ALL: Yeah, yeah, yeah!

Oh, Dear, What Can the Matter Be?

PRESENTATION SUGGESTIONS

The song for "Oh, Dear" is embedded in this script. You may wish to invite students to listen to the song (see below) several times before presenting the readers theatre script. This will help them learn the cadence and rhyme so that the song may be sung within the context of the script.

PROPS

No props are necessary for this script. However, if available, you may wish to have the narrator hold several blue ribbons during the presentation.

DELIVERY

The characters should act just a little worried during the presentation of their lines.

MUSICAL VERSION

Log on to the following Web Site for a musical version of this song: http://www.kididdles.com/lyrics/o002.html.

This site includes the background music for the song. Invite students to listen to the music one or two times, and then assist them in singing the lyrics as an accompaniment to the music. (Note: The lyrics provided on the site are slightly different than those included in this readers theatre script.)

MOVEMENT/DANCE

Arrange the students into a large circle. Select one student and invite him or her to slowly walk around the inside perimeter of the circle as the song is being sung by the entire class. The selected individual can put his or her hands to the sides of his or her face to denote a worried expression as he or she is walking. Ask the class to sing the song a second time, but now invite two individuals to walk around the inside perimeter of the circle. Repeat with three, four, and five individuals.

Oh, dear, what can the matter be?
Oh, dear, what can the matter be?
Oh, dear, what can the matter be?
Johnny's so long at the fair.

He promised to buy me a bunch of blue ribbons,
He promised to buy me a bunch of blue ribbons,
He promised to buy me a bunch of blue ribbons,
To bind up my bonnie brown hair.

Oh, dear, what can the matter be?
Oh, dear, what can the matter be?
Oh, dear, what can the matter be?
Johnny's so long at the fair.

Oh, Dear, What Can the Matter Be?

STAGING: The characters can all be seated on stools or chairs. Note that the narrator has two short parts in this script. The three main characters can be all girls, although that is not a requirement for this production.

Alex	April	Alicia	
X	X	X	
			Narrator
			X

NARRATOR: Welcome to our story. This is a sad story. It's not a happy story. Let's listen and see why.

ALEX: Oh, dear

APRIL: What do you mean, "Oh, dear?"

ALEX: I mean, oh, dear.

ALICIA: I don't get it.

ALEX: Well, I'm worried.

APRIL: Why are you worried?

ALEX: I'm worried about Johnny.

ALICIA: Why are you worried about Johnny?

APRIL: Did he do something wrong?

ALEX: No.

ALICIA: Is he lost?

ALEX: No.

APRIL: Did he forget something?

ALEX: No.

From *Songs and Rhymes Readers Theatre for Beginning Readers* by Anthony D. Fredericks. Westport, CT: Teacher Ideas Press. Copyright © 2008.

ALICIA: Then why are you worried?

ALEX: I'm worried because he went to the fair.

APRIL: That sounds like fun. Why would you be worried?

ALEX: Well, I'm worried because he has been there a long time.

ALICIA: Maybe he's just having fun.

APRIL: Yeah, maybe he's just having fun.

ALICIA: If I were at the fair, I'd have fun, too.

APRIL: Yeah, me too.

ALEX: But he's been there a long time.

ALICIA: How long?

ALEX: A really, really long time.

APRIL: Maybe he got lost.

ALICIA: Maybe he ate a lot of ice cream.

ALEX: No, I don't think so.

APRIL: Why not?

ALEX: Because he went to the fair to get me some ribbons.

ALICIA: Some ribbons!

ALEX: Yes, some ribbons.

APRIL: Why do you want some ribbons?

ALEX: So I can tie up my hair.

ALICIA: Oh.

ALEX: I'm still worried. I don't know what to do.

APRIL: I know what we can do.

ALEX: What?

APRIL: Well, we can sing a song.

ALEX: Sing a song!

ALICIA: Yes, we can sing a song. If we sing a song, maybe Johnny will come back.

ALEX: You know, I like that idea.

APRIL: So do I!

ALICIA: So do I!

NARRATOR: And, so, our three friends here are going to sing. They will sing the story about Johnny. Here goes.

ALEX: Oh, dear, what can the matter be?

APRIL: Oh, dear, what can the matter be?

ALICIA: Oh, dear, what can the matter be?

ALL: Johnny's so long at the fair.

ALEX: He promised to buy me a bunch of blue ribbons.

APRIL: He promised to buy her a bunch of blue ribbons.

ALICIA: He promised to buy her a bunch of blue ribbons.

ALL: To bind up her bonnie brown hair.

ALEX: Oh, dear, what can the matter be?

APRIL: Oh, dear, what can the matter be?

ALICIA: Oh, dear, what can the matter be?

ALL: Johnny's so long at the fair.

The Bear Went Over the Mountain

PRESENTATION SUGGESTIONS

Present the readers theatre script first and then invite students to sing the accompanying song. You may wish to have students practice the song first, then listen to the production, then sing the song as the conclusion to the entire production.

PROPS

A stuffed bear can be placed on a small table in the middle of the staging area.

DELIVERY

The narrator gets progressively angrier and angrier as the presentation progresses. The other characters should say their lines as though they are confused and unsure of what is happening. Toward the end of the script the narrator reaches a point of absolute frustration.

MUSICAL VERSION

Log on to the following Web site for a version of this song. The music is the same as that used for the song "For He's a Jolly Good Fellow": http://www.niehs.nih.gov/kids/lyrics/bearwent.htm.

MOVEMENT/DANCE

The entire group of students can sing this song together. Arrange the students into a large circle. For each verse, one student steps into the middle of the circle and performs the designated movements:

The bear went over the mountain, the bear went over the mountain. [Simulate walking.]
The bear went over the mountain, to see what he could see. [Hand shading eyes.]
And all that he could see, and all that he could see, [Hand shading eyes.]
Was the other side of the mountain, the other side of the mountain, [Pointing.]
The other side of the mountain, was all that he could see. [Shrug shoulders.]

The bear went over the river, the bear went over the river, [Simulate walking.]
The bear went over the river, to see what he could see. [Hand shading eyes.]
And all that he could see, and all that he could see, [Hand shading eyes.]
Was the other side of the river, the other side of the river, [Pointing.]
The other side of the river, was all that he could see. [Shrug shoulders.]

The bear went over the canyon, the bear went over the canyon. [Simulate walking.]
The bear went over the canyon, to see what he could see. [Hand shading eyes.]
And all that he could see, and all that he could see [Hand shading eyes.]
Was the other side of the canyon, the other side of the canyon, [pointing.]
The other side of the canyon, was all that he could see. [Shrug shoulders.]

The bear went over the desert, the bear went over the desert. [Simulate walking.]
The bear went over the desert, to see what he could see. [Hand shading eyes.]
And all that he could see, and all that he could see, [Hand shading eyes.]
Was the other side of the desert, the other side of the desert. [Pointing.]
The other side of the desert, was all that he could see. [Shrug shoulders.]

The bear went over the mountain, the bear went over the mountain. [Simulate walking.]
The bear went over the mountain, to see what he could see. [Hand shading eyes.]
And all that he could see, and all that he could see, [Hand shading eyes.]
Was the other side of the mountain, the other side of the mountain. [pointing.]
The other side of the mountain, was all that he could see. [Shrug shoulders.]

The Bear Went Over the Mountain

STAGING: The narrator can be placed on a tall stool to the side of the staging area. The characters can be on chairs or can be standing throughout the production.

```
        Mario                                      Heidi
          X              Becky             Matt      X
                           X      Thomas    X
                                    X
                                                     Narrator
                                                        X
```

NARRATOR: Once there was a bear.

MARIO: Wait! Did you say "bear?"

NARRATOR: Yes, I did.

MARIO: Hey, bears are dangerous.

NARRATOR: Yes, some can be.

BECKY: Is your bear dangerous?

NARRATOR: He's not my bear.

THOMAS: Then whose bear is he?

NARRATOR: I don't know. I'm just telling this story.

MATT: Where did the bear come from?

NARRATOR: I don't know. Maybe a zoo.

HEIDI: Do bears live at the zoo?

NARRATOR: Yes, they do. I don't know if this bear lived in a zoo.

MARIO: If he didn't live at the zoo, where did he live?

From *Songs and Rhymes Readers Theatre for Beginning Readers* by Anthony D. Fredericks. Westport, CT: Teacher Ideas Press. Copyright © 2008.

NARRATOR: I don't know. I'm just telling the story. I really don't know the bear.

BECKY: If you don't know the bear, how can you tell the story?

NARRATOR: You don't have to know a bear to tell a bear story.

THOMAS: What do you have to know?

NARRATOR: You have to know about storytelling.

MATT: You mean, you don't have to know about bears?

NARRATOR: I guess not.

HEIDI: How can you know about stories and not know about bears?

NARRATOR: Because I know stories. I don't know about bears.

MARIO: If you don't know about bears, then how can you tell a bear story?

NARRATOR: Because I know about stories.

BECKY: Not bears?

NARRATOR: No, not bears.

THOMAS: So, where did this bear come from?

NARRATOR: I DON'T KNOW!!!

MATT: This is a strange story. He [points] doesn't know any bears.

NARRATOR: I don't know about bears. And I don't know about giraffes. Or elephants. Or zebras either.

HEIDI: Oh, are you going to tell us a story about zebras? I like zebras.

NARRATOR: NO, I'm not going to tell a story about zebras. I'm going to tell a story about a bear.

MARIO: What happened to the zebras?

NARRATOR: Nothing happened to the zebras. They aren't even in the story.

BECKY: Oh, you mean the story about the bear?

NARRATOR: Yes, the stupid story about the stupid bear.

THOMAS: I didn't know the bear was stupid.

NARRATOR: The bear isn't stupid. This whole thing is getting stupid.

MATT: Oh, are you saying that we are stupid?

NARRATOR: No. I'm not. I just think I'm going crazy.

HEIDI: So now we have a stupid and crazy storyteller. Or maybe we have a stupid and crazy bear.

NARRATOR: NO, NO, NO!!! Just forget the whole thing. Let's just listen to the stupid song. No, I mean let's just listen to the song. OK?

ALL: OK!

[Play the music and invite all the students to sing the song.]

Rock-a-Bye Baby

PRESENTATION SUGGESTIONS

The characters should turn and face each other as they are speaking. The baby should occasionally look over his or her shoulder to talk to the other characters. The narrator speaks exclusively to the baby.

PROPS

You may wish to provide the baby with a bonnet, a stuffed animal, a rattle, or some other baby item to hold throughout the production. If possible, bring in a small tree branch for the characters to point to.

DELIVERY

The characters should all be having a comfortable conversation—similar to what they might have on the playground or at recess.

MUSICAL VERSION

Log on to the following Web site for a slow-paced and easy-to-follow version of this ever-popular song: http://www.niehs.nih.gov/kids/lyrics/rockaby.htm.

MOVEMENT/DANCE

Invite the entire class to share the following song and movements as the conclusion to this readers theatre production. Have students listen to the music one or two times and then practice singing the words along with the music. Afterward they can add the designated movements.

Rock-a-bye, baby
[Hold arms together in front of body and swing them from side to side.]
In the treetop. [Point upwards.]
When the wind blows, [Blow with mouth.]
The cradle will rock.
[Hold arms together in front of body and swing them from side to side.]
When the bough breaks,
[Use both hands to simulate a breaking motion.]
The cradle will fall,
[Hold hands high, then drop suddenly.]
And down will come baby, [Simulate crying.]
Cradle and all.
[Hold arms together in front of body and swing them from side to side.]
[Repeat.]

Rock-a-Bye Baby

STAGING: The narrator and the four characters all sit on stools or chairs. The baby sits on the floor cross-legged.

```
Narrator
X                        Roland        Lani
                           X             X
              Terry                            Cory
                X                               X
Baby
X
```

NARRATOR: Once upon a time there was a baby.

BABY: That's me.

NARRATOR: This was a special baby. This baby could talk.

BABY: I'm very smart.

NARRATOR: This talking baby had some adventures.

BABY: Yes, I had some adventures.

NARRATOR: Maybe we should let our friends [points to other characters] tell the story of the very smart baby.

BABY: That's me!

TERRY: OK, here we go.

ROLAND: One day, the baby was sleeping in his bed.

LANI: He was sound asleep.

CORY: Then something happened.

TERRY: Yes, something amazing happened.

ROLAND: Somehow the baby got into a tree.

LANI: How did the baby get into a tree?

CORY: I don't know. Maybe he flew there.

TERRY: No, that isn't right. Babies can't fly.

ROLAND: Then how did he get up in the tree?

LANI: Maybe a bird put him there.

CORY: No, I don't think so.

TERRY: Well, I just don't know.

ROLAND: Maybe the author of the story just put the baby there.

LANI: Yeah, authors do things like that.

CORY: Yeah, authors are weird sometimes.

TERRY: They do strange things sometimes.

ROLAND: Like put babies in the tops of trees.

LANI: Yeah, those authors are weird.

CORY: Isn't it dangerous in the tree?

TERRY: Yes, it is.

ROLAND: What could happen to the baby?

LANI: He could live in a bird's nest.

CORY: Or he could swing in the tree like a monkey.

TERRY: I don't think so.

ROLAND: Neither do I.

LANI: But it's still dangerous.

CORY: Yes, it is.

TERRY: The bough could break.

ROLAND: Hey, what's a bough?

LANI: A bough is another word for "branch."

CORY: Oh, so a bough and a branch are the same thing?

TERRY: Right.

ROLAND: So what does that mean.

LANI: Well if the wind blows, then the bough might break.

CORY: Then what would happen?

TERRY: Well, our baby friend here [points to Baby] might fall.

ROLAND: Wow, that would be awful.

LANI: You bet!

CORY: The baby might fall on the ground.

TERRY: That would hurt.

ROLAND: That wouldn't be fun.

LANI: No, it wouldn't.

CORY: So what should we do?

BABY: I have an idea.

NARRATOR: What's that?

BABY: Well, maybe you guys should sing a song.

NARRATOR: Sing a song?

BABY: Yeah. If you sing a song I'll go to sleep.

NARRATOR: And then what?

BABY: If I'm asleep, then I won't have any problems.

NARRATOR: Problems?

BABY: Yes, problems like flying up into a tree. Or living in a bird's nest. Or falling from a bough or a branch.

NARRATOR: That sounds great. So let's sing the song.

BABY: I like that idea.

NARRATOR: Then here we go!

[Play the music and invite students to sing the song. You may wish to have them perform the movements indicated in the "Movement/Dance" section on page 87.]

Three Blind Mice

PRESENTATION SUGGESTIONS

In this presentation the song is a separate entity. You may wish to have students put on the readers theatre production first and then listen to the song (below). Afterward the entire class can sing the song together using the suggested movements.

PROPS

You may wish to provide each of the "mice" with a set of sunglasses (to indicate their blindness). This is not necessary, however.

DELIVERY

The narrator should present his or her lines in a matter-of-fact way. "Nancy" and "Debbie" can speak in an excited and animated fashion. "Jan" is a smart-aleck and should speak her lines as a jokester would.

MUSICAL VERSION

Log on to the following Web site for a musical version of this classical rhyme: http://www.niehs. nih.gov/kids/lyrics/blindmic.htm.

MOVEMENT/DANCE

Invite one student to take on the role of the farmer's wife. Provide this individual with a plastic ruler (to simulate a carving knife). All the other students can take on the roles of the blind mice (with the accompanying movements).

Three blind mice, [Hands over eyes.]
Three blind mice. [Hands over eyes.]
See how they run,
[Simulate running in place.]
See how they run!
[Simulate running in place.]

They all ran after
[Simulate running in place.]
The farmer's wife. [Point to "wife."]
She cut off their tails
["Wife" simulates chopping motion.]
With a carving knife.
["Wife" holds up ruler or flat of hand.]

Did you ever see
[Hands, facing outward, on side of eyes.]
Such a sight in your life
[Everyone point to everyone else.]
As three blind mice? [Hands over eyes.]

Three Blind Mice

STAGING: The narrator can sit on a stool to the front and side of the characters. The characters should be standing throughout the presentation. They may be placed at music stands or hold their scripts in their hands.

```
                              Debbie
                                X
                 Nancy                      Jan
                   X                         X
   Narrator
      X
```

NARRATOR: Once upon a time there were these three mice.

NANCY: That's me!

DEBBIE: . . . and me!

JAN: . . . and me!

NARRATOR: Anyway . . . these three mice lived on a farm.

NANCY: There were cows on the farm.

DEBBIE: There were pigs on the farm.

JAN: There was lots of stinky stuff on the farm.

NARRATOR: As I was saying . . . . These three mice lived on a farm. But the people who lived on the farm didn't like mice.

NANCY: They didn't like us.

DEBBIE: Yes, they didn't like us.

JAN: I don't know why. But they didn't like us.

NANCY: Was it something we said?

DEBBIE: Was it something we ate?

JAN: Was it something we did?

From *Songs and Rhymes Readers Theatre for Beginning Readers* by Anthony D. Fredericks. Westport, CT: Teacher Ideas Press. Copyright © 2008.

NARRATOR: I think it was just because you were mice.

NANCY: What do you mean?

DEBBIE: You mean, people don't like mice?

JAN: You mean, people don't like cute mice? Like us?

NARRATOR: That's it. Some people don't like mice. They think mice are bad.

NANCY: We're not bad.

DEBBIE: We're not bad at all.

JAN: We're really very cute.

NARRATOR: That may be. But some people don't like you.

NANCY: Maybe we don't like them.

DEBBIE: Yeah, maybe we don't like them.

JAN: Yeah, whatever they said.

NARRATOR: So the wife was always looking for the mice. She didn't like the mice. She wanted to hurt them.

NANCY: She isn't a very nice person.

DEBBIE: Yeah, she's really bad.

JAN: Maybe we don't like her either.

NARRATOR: The farmer's wife would walk around all day. She was always looking for our mice friends here. [points to characters]

NANCY: I bet she was dangerous.

DEBBIE: Yeah, she wanted to hurt us.

JAN: Yeah, who wants to hurt cute mice like us?

NARRATOR: The wife walked around with a knife. She had a really sharp knife.

NANCY: She really is dangerous.

DEBBIE: A knife! A knife!! A knife!!!

JAN: I don't think I like this person.

NARRATOR: So she would have a knife. She would always look for the mice. One day she saw them.

NANCY: She saw us all right.

DEBBIE: Boy, were we scared.

JAN: Yeah, that old lady had a sharp knife. We were scared.

NARRATOR: And the old woman ran after the mice. She wanted to do something very bad. She wanted to cut off their tails.

NANCY: Oh, no!

DEBBIE: Oh, no!! Oh, no!!

JAN: Oh, no!!! Oh, no!!! Oh, no!!!

NARRATOR: The farmer's wife ran after the mice. The mice ran away from the farmer's wife. They ran around and around the house.

NANCY: Yes, she chased us all over the house.

DEBBIE: We ran real fast.

JAN: We wanted to get away from that crazy lady.

NARRATOR: The farmer's wife chased the mice. The mice ran away. There was lot's of chasing and lots of running.

NANCY: The wife chased us.

DEBBIE: We ran away.

JAN: It was horrible!

NARRATOR: Finally everybody got tired. They all stopped. They decided to be friends.

NANCY: Yeah, we decided to be friends.

DEBBIE: We decided we were hungry.

JAN: We decided we all wanted some chocolate chip ice cream.

NARRATOR: Well, that's not really what happened. You must listen to the song. Then you'll know what really happened.

ALL: Good bye.

Row, Row, Row Your Boat

PRESENTATION SUGGESTIONS

This script uses a song that may be familiar to many students. The song is presented three different ways within the script. It is not necessary to introduce the song before the script is presented.

PROPS

No props are necessary for this script.

DELIVERY

The characters are simply designated as "Person A," "Person B," etc. You may wish to have the characters use their own names, too. The delivery should be upbeat and light.

MUSICAL VERSION

Log on to the following Web site for a slow and easy-to-follow version of the song: http://www. songsforteaching.com/folk/rowrowrowyourboat.htm.

Click on "Listen to this song" to hear the song. You may wish to invite children to listen to the music in advance of the script. Or you may wish to have students listen to the song after they have presented the script. When students are comfortable with the lyrics, invite them to sing along.

MOVEMENT/DANCE

Place four chairs in a line (one behind the other). Put one student in each chair. Lay some blue ribbons on the floor on either side of the chairs. Invite each student to imagine that he or she has an oar in his or her hands. (If students are not familiar with rowing, show them some illustrations beforehand.) These students can simulate the rowing action down a stream (the ribbons) as the song or lyrics are said by the teacher or other students in the class.

Row, row, row your boat,
[Students simulate rowing.]
Gently down the stream.
[Wiggle the blue ribbons back and forth on the floor.]
Merrily, merrily, merrily, merrily,
[Rowers will turn and smile at the audience.]
Life is but a dream.
[Lift the ribbons high overhead and wiggle them back and forth.]

[Repeat.]

Row, Row, Row Your Boat

STAGING: The characters can be seated on stools or chairs in a straight line across the staging area.

Narrator	Person A	Person B	Person C	Person D
X	X	X	X	X

NARRATOR: Once upon a time there was a boy. He liked to row. He liked to row his boat. He liked to row, row his boat. He liked to row, row, row, his boat. So, he sang a song. Here is the song. Listen.

PERSON A: Row,

PERSON B: Row,

PERSON C: Row

PERSON D: Your boat.

PERSON A: Gently

PERSON B: Down

PERSON C: The

PERSON D: Stream.

PERSON A: Merrily,

PERSON B: Merrily,

PERSON C: Merrily,

PERSON D: Merrily.

PERSON A: Life

PERSON B: Is

PERSON C: But

PERSON D: A dream.

PERSON A: Hey, that was fun!

PERSON B: Yes, it was!

PERSON C: Let's do it again.

PERSON D: Yeah, let's!

NARRATOR: Why don't you do it differently?

PERSON A: What do you mean?

PERSON B: Yeah, what do you mean?

NARRATOR: Well, each of you could do one whole line.

PERSON C: Hey, that sounds like fun.

PERSON D: Well then, let's do it!

NARRATOR: Is everybody ready? OK. let's do it.

PERSON A: Row, row, row, your boat.

PERSON B: Gently down the stream.

PERSON C: Merrily, merrily, merrily, merrily,

PERSON D: Life is but a dream.

NARRATOR: Everybody did a good job.

PERSON A: Yes, we did!

PERSON B: We sure did!

NARRATOR: Let's have the audience help us.

PERSON C: How can we do that?

NARRATOR: Each of you can start a line. But stop before saying the last word. Point to the audience [points to the audience]. Then let them say the last word.

PERSON D: That sounds like fun. Let's do it.

NARRATOR: OK, are you [points to audience] ready? Then, let's go.

PERSON A: Row, row, row your . . .

AUDIENCE: . . . boat.

PERSON B: Gently down the . . .

AUDIENCE: . . . stream.

PERSON C: Merrily, merrily, merrily, . . .

AUDIENCE: Merrily.

PERSON D: Life is but a . . . .

AUDIENCE: Dream.

NARRATOR: Very good. Everybody did a good job!

AUDIENCE: Yeah! Yeah! Yeah!

B-I-N-G-O

PRESENTATION SUGGESTIONS

This script uses the actual song embedded in another story. Prior to performing the script you may wish to play the music for the students so that they are used to the tempo and cadence of the song. Invite the performers and the audience to sing their parts instead of just saying them.

PROPS

If possible, obtain a stuffed dog (or some other toy dog) to place in the center of the staging area.

DELIVERY

The characters and the audience should sing their parts throughout the production. Many youngsters will be familiar with this song, but others may not. It may be necessary to teach the song (and the accompanying clapping) to students in advance of any production.

MUSICAL VERSION

Log on to the following Web site for a sprightly and lively version of this popular summer camp song: http://www.niehs.nih.gov/kids/lyrics/bingo.htm.

MOVEMENT/DANCE

This readers theatre script is a good example of how movements can be easily incorporated into any script. The entire production is a series of movements on the part of the players as well as the audience. Be sure the audience members are aware of their integral part in this production. You may wish to provide some initial practice in the accumulating clapping sequence that is so much a part of this song.

B-I-N-G-O

STAGING: The characters can be standing or seated on chairs. They may also be placed at individual lecterns.

Narrator					
X					
	B	I	N	G	O
	X	X	X	X	X

NARRATOR: Once upon a time there was this farmer.

B: OK, so there was this farmer.

I: Yeah, what's the big deal? A farmer.

N: Everybody knows what a farmer is.

G: Everybody here [points to audience] knows what a farmer is. They also know what a farmer does.

O: [to narrator] So why are you telling us about a farmer?

NARRATOR: Well, I was getting to that. You see this farmer had a very special dog.

B: Lots of farmers have dogs.

I: They have cows and pigs, too.

N: And chickens and geese.

G: And horses and cats.

O: Yeah, farmers have lots and lots of animals.

NARRATOR: Well, this farmer had a dog. And the dog's name was Bingo.

B: That's a funny name for a dog.

I: That would be a funny name for a cat.

N: And a funny name for a cow.

G: Or any animal.

O: OK, so we have this dog. He has the funny name of Bingo. What next?

NARRATOR: I was just getting to that. Anyway, the farmer wrote a song about his dog.

B: You mean the farmer was a writer?

I: Just like the person who wrote this play?

N: He must have been very very smart.

G: Just like the person who wrote this play!

O: I guess farmers can do many things. Many things besides milking cows.

NARRATOR: One day the farmer shared his song. He shared it with his friends and neighbors. And everybody started singing the song. And the song made everybody happy. So the farmer wanted to share this song with you [points to audience].

B: Are we going to sing the "Bingo" song?

I: I guess we're singing the song for them [points to audience].

N: This should be fun.

G: We hope you have fun with us.

O: Are you [points to audience] ready? We are. Let's go. OK, Narrator, you can start us off.

NARRATOR: There was a farmer had a dog,

ALL: And Bingo was his name-o.

AUDIENCE: B-I-N-G-O!
B-I-N-G-O!
B-I-N-G-O!

ALL: And Bingo was his name-o!

NARRATOR: There was a farmer had a dog,

B: And Bingo was his name-o.

AUDIENCE: [Clap]-I-N-G-O!
[Clap]-I-N-G-O!
[Clap]-I-N-G-O!

B: And Bingo was his name-o!

NARRATOR: There was a farmer had a dog,

I: And Bingo was his name-o.

AUDIENCE: [Clap, clap]-N-G-O!
[Clap, clap]-N-G-O!
[Clap, clap]-N-G-O!

I: And Bingo was his name-o!

NARRATOR: There was a farmer had a dog,

N: And Bingo was his name-o.

AUDIENCE: [Clap, clap, clap]-G-O!
[Clap, clap, clap]-G-O!
[Clap, clap, clap]-G-O!

N: And Bingo was his name-o!

NARRATOR: There was a farmer had a dog,

G: And Bingo was his name-o.

AUDIENCE: [Clap, clap, clap, clap]-O!
[Clap, clap, clap, clap]-O!
[Clap, clap, clap, clap]-O!

G: And Bingo was his name-o!

NARRATOR: There was a farmer had a dog,

O: And Bingo was his name-o.

AUDIENCE: [Clap, clap, clap, clap, clap]
[Clap, clap, clap, clap, clap]
[Clap, clap, clap, clap, clap]

O: And Bingo was his name-o!

NARRATOR: That was great. That was a lot of fun. Let's do it again. This time we'll do it with music. OK?

ALL: OK. Let's go!

[Invite students to sing the B-I-N-G-O song in time with the music]

NARRATOR: There was a farmer had a dog,

ALL: And Bingo was his name-o.

AUDIENCE: B-I-N-G-O!
B-I-N-G-O!
B-I-N-G-O!

ALL: And Bingo was his name-o!

NARRATOR: There was a farmer had a dog,

B: And Bingo was his name-o.

AUDIENCE: [Clap]-I-N-G-O!
[Clap]-I-N-G-O!
[Clap]-I-N-G-O!

B: And Bingo was his name-o!

NARRATOR: There was a farmer had a dog,

I: And Bingo was his name-o.

AUDIENCE: [Clap, clap]-N-G-O!
[Clap, clap]-N-G-O!
[Clap, clap]-N-G-O!

I: And Bingo was his name-o!

NARRATOR: There was a farmer had a dog,

N: And Bingo was his name-o.

AUDIENCE: [Clap, clap, clap]-G-O!
[Clap, clap, clap]-G-O!
[Clap, clap, clap]-G-O!

N: And Bingo was his name-o!

NARRATOR: There was a farmer had a dog,

G: And Bingo was his name-o.

AUDIENCE: [Clap, clap, clap, clap]-O!
[Clap, clap, clap, clap]-O!
[Clap, clap, clap, clap]-O!

G: And Bingo was his name-o!

NARRATOR: There was a farmer had a dog,

O: And Bingo was his name-o.

AUDIENCE: [Clap, clap, clap, clap, clap]
[Clap, clap, clap, clap, clap]
[Clap, clap, clap, clap, clap]

O: And Bingo was his name-o!

Skip to My Lou

PRESENTATION SUGGESTIONS

There are many ways in which your students can present this script. You may wish to have them do it without the music or with the accompanying music (see below). It is suggested that you play the song several times through so that students unfamiliar with the song can get a feel for the rhythm and cadence of the lyrics.

PROPS

There are no props necessary for this script.

DELIVERY

The presentation should be upbeat and light. Lots of singing is encouraged; or a combination of speaking and singing can be used.

MUSICAL VERSION

Log on to the following Web site for an easy-to-follow musical version of this song: http://www. niehs.nih.gov/kids/lyrics/skipto.htm.

This Web site plays the song over and over. You may wish to have children listen to the song several times before launching into their initial presentation of the script.

MOVEMENT/DANCE

This version of the song should be done by the entire class. On the other hand, you may wish to divide the class into two or three separate groups and invite each group to perform the movements individually.

Place students in a circle and invite them to move in a counterclockwise motion (as indicated).

Fly's in the buttermilk,
[Point to the interior of the circle.]
Shoo, fly, shoo.
[Move hands in an underhand waving motion.]
Fly's in the buttermilk,
[Point to the interior of the circle.]
Shoo, fly, shoo,
[Move hands in an underhand waving motion.]
Fly's in the buttermilk.
[Point to the interior of the circle.]
Shoo, fly, shoo.
[Move hands in an underhand waving motion.]
Skip to my Lou, my darlin'.

Skip, skip, skip to my Lou,
[Skip in a counterclockwise motion.]
Skip, skip, skip to my Lou,
[Repeat.]
Skip, skip, skip to my Lou,
[Repeat.]
Skip to my Lou, my darlin'.
[Repeat.]

Cat's in the cream jar,
[Put hands on the side of face and wiggle fingers.]
Ooh, ooh, ooh.
[Shake the index finger back and forth.]
Cat's in the cream jar,
[Put hands on the side of face and wiggle fingers.]
Ooh, ooh, ooh.
[Shake the index finger back and forth.]
Cat's in the cream jar,
[Put hands on the side of face and wiggle fingers.]
Ooh, ooh, ooh.
[Shake the index finger back and forth.]
Skip to my Lou, my darlin'.

Skip, skip, skip to my Lou,
[Skip in a counterclockwise motion.]
Skip, skip, skip to my Lou,
[Repeat.]
Skip, skip, skip to my Lou,
[Repeat.]
Skip to my Lou, my darlin'.
[Repeat.]

Off to Texas,
[Take large step into circle and then back.]
Two by two.
[Hold up two fingers on each hand.]
Off to Texas,
[Take large step into circle and then back.]
Two by two.
[Hold up two fingers on each hand.]
Off to Texas,
[Take large step into circle and then back.]
Two by two.
[Hold up two fingers on each hand.]
Skip to my Lou, my darlin'.

Skip, skip, skip to my Lou,
[Skip in a counterclockwise motion.]
Skip, skip, skip to my Lou,
[Repeat.]
Skip, skip, skip to my Lou,
[Repeat.]
Skip to my Lou, my darlin'.
[Repeat.]

Skip to My Lou

STAGING:

❖ **Version 1:** The characters should all be standing in a loose circle. Each character should have an individual copy of the script. The entire group moves in a counterclockwise circle as the lines are being read.

❖ **Version 2:** Use the "staging" in the example above. This time the characters say their lines in tune with the accompanying music.

❖ **Version 3:** Invite a pair of students to say each line as the group moves in a counterclockwise circle. (NOTE: This will take some practice but can be a lot of fun for everyone).

NOTE: There is no narrator for this script. There are lyrics in which the entire group of six characters speak in unison. These lyrics can be spoken by the characters or can be assigned to the audience.

```
                        Number 1
                           X
         Number 6                      Number 2
            X                             X
         Number 5                      Number 3
            X                             X
                        Number 4
                           X
```

NUMBER 1: Fly's in the buttermilk,

NUMBER 2: Shoo, fly, shoo.

NUMBER 3: Fly's in the buttermilk,

NUMBER 4: Shoo, fly, shoo.

NUMBER 5: Fly's in the buttermilk,

NUMBER 6: Shoo, fly, shoo.

ALL: Skip to my Lou, my darlin'.

ALL [singing]: Skip, skip, skip to my Lou,
Skip, skip, skip to my Lou,
Skip, skip, skip to my Lou,
Skip to my Lou, my darlin'.

From *Songs and Rhymes Readers Theatre for Beginning Readers* by Anthony D. Fredericks. Westport, CT: Teacher Ideas Press. Copyright © 2008.

NUMBER 1:   Cat's in the cream jar,

NUMBER 2:   Ooh, ooh, ooh.

NUMBER 3:   Cat's in the cream jar,

NUMBER 4:   Ooh, ooh, ooh.

NUMBER 5:   Cat's in the cream jar,

NUMBER 6:   Ooh, ooh, ooh.

ALL: Skip to my Lou, my darlin'.

ALL [singing]:   Skip, skip, skip to my Lou,
Skip, skip, skip to my Lou,
Skip, skip, skip to my Lou,
Skip to my Lou, my darlin'.

NUMBER 1:   Off to Texas,

NUMBER 2:   Two by two.

NUMBER 3:   Off to Texas,

NUMBER 4:   Two by two.

NUMBER 5:   Off to Texas,

NUMBER 6:   Two by two.

ALL: Skip to my Lou, my darlin'.

ALL [singing]:   Skip, skip, skip to my Lou,
Skip, skip, skip to my Lou,
Skip, skip, skip to my Lou,
Skip to my Lou, my darlin'.

A Tisket, a Tasket

PRESENTATION SUGGESTIONS

This script uses the nursery rhyme "A Tisket, a Tasket" embedded in another story. It would be advantageous to introduce this song to students in advance of a readers theatre presentation. That will help youngsters get used to the "sing-song" nature of this rhyme—something they may wish to interject into their presentation of the script.

PROPS

If possible, obtain a small basket (an Easter basket, for example). Tie some green and yellow ribbons onto the basket and place it in the center of the staging area. Additional props (see "Movement/Dance" below) can be obtained and used for a class sing-along.

DELIVERY

The characters should present this script in a light and casual fashion. You may want to play some accompanying music in the background.

MUSICAL VERSION

Log on to the following web site for a musical version of this well-known nursery rhyme: http://www.bussongs.com/songs/a_tisket_a_tasket_short.php

Click on the "Play" button and listen to the musical version several times with students. When students are comfortable with the music, invite them to sing the song along with the music.

MOVEMENT/DANCE

Designate two students as separate characters for this presentation. Play the music in the background and invite other students to sing the song while these two characters are performing the designated motions. Provide opportunities for other students to take on these roles.

A tisket, a tasket,
[Two students skip in a circle around the basket.]
A green and yellow basket.
[As students skip, they point to the basket.]
I wrote a letter to my love.
[Students stop skipping; one student takes a piece of paper and a pencil and simulates the writing of a letter.]
And on the way, I dropped it.
[The students resume their skipping, but the letter-writer drops the piece of paper on the floor.]

I dropped it, I dropped it.
[The student stops and points to the paper.]
And on the way, I dropped it,
[Both students point to the paper on the floor.]
A little boy picked it up,
[A third student comes in from offstage and picks up the paper.].
And put it in his pocket.
[The third student puts the paper in his or her (imaginary) pocket.]

A Tisket, a Tasket

STAGING: The characters can all be seated on stools or chairs. They may also be standing or placed at individual lecterns. The narrator should be placed off to one side of the staging area.

```
                                        Max
                                         X
                            Molly
                              X                      Mary
                                                      X
                   Maria
                     X
          Narrator
             X
```

NARRATOR:	Hello, my name is Narrator.
MARIA:	Gee, that's a funny name.
MOLLY:	Yeah, who gave you that name?
NARRATOR:	I don't know.
MAX:	It's still a funny name.
MARY:	Yeah, it is a very funny name.
NARRATOR:	Well, it says right here [points to script] that it is my name.
MARIA:	So someone else gave you that name?
NARRATOR:	Yeah, I guess so.
MOLLY:	That person is strange.
MAX:	Yeah, he sure is strange.
MARY:	I wonder what his name is?
NARRATOR:	I think his name is "Author."
MARIA:	Wow, that's a strange name, too.
MOLLY:	You bet. It's a very strange name.

From *Songs and Rhymes Readers Theatre for Beginning Readers* by Anthony D. Fredericks. Westport, CT: Teacher Ideas Press. Copyright © 2008.

MAX: He must be a very strange person.

MARY: Yes, he must be.

NARRATOR: OK, let's stop with the names. Let's start with the story.

MARIA: OK, that sounds like fun!

MOLLY: Yes it does.

MAX: I'm ready.

MARY: And so am I.

NARRATOR: OK, then let's go. Maria, you can get us started.

MARIA: A tisket,

MOLLY: A tasket,

MAX: A green . . .

MARY: . . . and yellow basket,

MARIA: I wrote a letter . . .

MOLLY: . . . to my love.

MAX: And on the way . . .

MARY: . . . I dropped it.

MARIA: I dropped it,

MOLLY: I dropped it,

MAX: And on the way . . .

MARY: I dropped it.

MARIA: A little boy . . .

MOLLY: . . . picked it up,

MAX: And put it . . .

MARY: . . . in his pocket.

MARIA: That is a funny story.

MOLLY: Yes, it is a very funny story.

MAX: It's as funny as your name [points to narrator].

MARY: And it's as funny as the name of the person who wrote this story.

NARRATOR: [to audience] And so this is the end of our funny story. There's just one thing I want to know.

MARIA: What's that?

MOLLY: Yeah, what's that?

NARRATOR: I want to know what a "tisket" is.

MAX: Yeah, that's a funny word.

NARRATOR: And what is a "tasket?"

MARY: I don't know. But those are both funny words.

NARRATOR: [to audience] We hope you enjoyed the funny words. And we hope you enjoyed our funny story.

ALL: Good-bye! [waving]

This Old Man

PRESENTATION SUGGESTIONS

This script has the song lyrics embedded in the presentation. You may wish to introduce the song to students in advance of the readers theatre presentation. Invite the audience to sing the song (accompanied by the music) at the end of the presentation.

PROPS

No props are necessary for this production.

DELIVERY

The delivery should be breezy and fun. The narrator can speak in a serious tone of voice, but the characters should all be inquisitive (at the beginning of the presentation) and full of life (during the reading of the song).

MUSICAL VERSION

Log on to the following Web site for a quick-paced version of this song: http://www.niehs.nih.gov/kids/lyrics/oldman.htm. (Note: You may wish to have students listen to the song several times in order to get used to the cadence and pace of the music.)

The song repeats itself over and over.

MOVEMENT/DANCE

Invite all the students to stand and perform the following movements as they sing and listen to the music. After students are comfortable with these movements, invite them to create their own for selected portions of the song.

This old man, he played one.
[Hold up one finger.]
He played knick-knack on my thumb.
[Tap thumb several times.]
With a knick-knack paddywhack, give a dog a bone,
[Put right hand out.]
This old man came rolling home.
[Roll hands over each other.]

This old man, he played two.
[Hold up two fingers.]
He played knick-knack on my shoe.
[Tap one shoe several times.]
With a knick-knack paddywhack, give a dog a bone,
[Put right hand out.]
This old man came rolling home.
[Roll hands over each other.]

This old man, he played three.
[Hold up three fingers.]
He played knick-knack on my knee.
[Tap knee several times.]
With a knick-knack paddywhack, give a dog a bone,
[Put right hand out.]
This old man came rolling home.
[Roll hands over each other.]

This old man, he played four.
[Hold up four fingers.]
He played knick-knack on my door.
[Tap on imaginary door.]
With a knick-knack paddywhack, give a dog a bone,
[Put right hand out.]
This old man came rolling home.
[Roll hands over each other.]

This old man, he played five.
[Hold up five fingers.]
He played knick-knack on my hive.
[Tap forehead several times.]
With a knick-knack paddywhack, give a dog a bone,
[Put right hand out.]
This old man came rolling home.
[Roll hands over each other.]

This old man, he played six.
[Hold up six fingers.]
He played knick-knack on my sticks.
[Tap fingers on opposite hand.]
With a knick-knack paddywhack, give a dog a bone,
[Put right hand out.]
This old man came rolling home.
[Roll hands over each other.]

This old man, he played seven.
[Hold up seven fingers.]
He played knick-knack up in heaven.
[Tap air over head.]
With a knick-knack paddywhack, give a dog a bone,
[Put right hand out.]
This old man came rolling home.
[Roll hands over each other.]

This old man, he played eight.
[Hold up eight fingers.]
He played knick-knack on my gate.
[Bend over and tap on imaginary gate.]
With a knick-knack paddywhack, give a dog a bone,
[Put right hand out.]
This old man came rolling home.
[Roll hands over each other.]

This old man, he played nine.
[Hold up nine fingers.]
He played knick-knack on my spine.
[Tap the spine of another person.]
With a knick-knack paddywhack, give a dog a bone,
[Put right hand out.]
This old man came rolling home.
[Roll hands over each other.]

This old man, he played ten.
[Hold up ten fingers.]
He played knick-knack on my hen,
[Everyone make chicken sounds.]
With a knick-knack paddywhack, give a dog a bone,
[Put right hand out.]
This old man came rolling home.
[Roll hands over each other.]

This Old Man

STAGING: The characters can be seated on stools or chairs. They may also be standing or placed at individual lecterns or music stands.

	Sam		Tammy	
Narrator	X		X	
X				
		Michael		April
		X		X

NARRATOR: Once upon a time there was this old man.

SAM: What did he do?

NARRATOR: Well, not much.

MICHAEL: What do you mean?

NARRATOR: Well, you see this old man played a lot.

TAMMY: He played a lot? You mean he played lots of games?

NARRATOR: Well, that's about it.

APRIL: That doesn't sound like much.

NARRATOR: It isn't. You see, he was an old man. He lived by himself.

SAM: Oh, so he didn't have any friends?

NARRATOR: Yeah, he had lots of friends. But he just liked to play by himself.

MICHAEL: I thought you needed to have other people if you were going to play any games.

NARRATOR: Well, this old man made up his own games.

TAMMY: Did he really invent his own games?

NARRATOR: That's right. He invented lots of new games.

APRIL: Can we play some of those games?

From *Songs and Rhymes Readers Theatre for Beginning Readers* by Anthony D. Fredericks. Westport, CT: Teacher Ideas Press. Copyright © 2008.

NARRATOR: I guess you can.

SAM: Can we do it right now?

NARRATOR: Here's something better. Why don't you tell everyone [points to audience] the story about the old man?

MICHAEL: That sounds like a neat idea!

TAMMY: Yeah, it sure does!

NARRATOR: OK, are you [points to characters] all ready?

APRIL: I think we are!

NARRATOR: OK, it's all yours!

SAM: This old man,

MICHAEL: He played one.

TAMMY: He played knick-knack on my thumb.

APRIL: With a knick-knack paddywhack, give a dog a bone,

ALL: This old man came rolling home.

MICHAEL: This old man,

TAMMY: He played two.

APRIL: He played knick-knack on my shoe.

SAM: With a knick-knack paddywhack, give a dog a bone,

ALL: This old man came rolling home.

TAMMY: This old man,

APRIL: He played three.

SAM: He played knick-knack on my knee.

MICHAEL: With a knick-knack paddywhack, give a dog a bone,

ALL: This old man came rolling home.

APRIL: This old man,

SAM: He played four.

MICHAEL: He played knick-knack on my door.

TAMMY: With a knick-knack paddywhack, give a dog a bone,

ALL: This old man came rolling home.

SAM: This old man,

MICHAEL: He played five.

TAMMY: He played knick-knack on my hive.

APRIL: With a knick-knack paddywhack, give a dog a bone,

ALL: This old man came rolling home.

MICHAEL: This old man,

TAMMY: He played six.

APRIL: He played knick-knack on my sticks.

SAM: With a knick-knack paddywhack, give a dog a bone,

ALL: This old man came rolling home.

TAMMY: This old man,

APRIL: He played seven.

SAM: He played knick-knack up in heaven.

MICHAEL: With a knick-knack paddywhack, give a dog a bone,

ALL: This old man came rolling home.

APRIL: This old man,

SAM: He played eight.

MICHAEL: He played knick-knack on my gate.

TAMMY: With a knick-knack paddywhack, give a dog a bone,

ALL: This old man came rolling home.

SAM: This old man,

MICHAEL: He played nine.

TAMMY: He played knick-knack on my spine.

APRIL: With a knick-knack paddywhack, give a dog a bone,

ALL: This old man came rolling home.

MICHAEL: This old man,

TAMMY: He played ten.

APRIL: He played knick-knack on my hen.

SAM: With a knick-knack paddywhack, give a dog a bone,

ALL: This old man came rolling home.

NARRATOR: Well, that's the end of our story.

SAM: That's right. We're all done.

MICHAEL: And the old man is done.

TAMMY: Good bye!

APRIL: Good bye!

ALL: Good bye! [waves to audience]

Do Your Ears Hang Low?

PRESENTATION SUGGESTIONS

This script can be presented with or without the accompanying music. After students have become comfortable with the lyrics, invite them to sing the song together as a class. This can be done after the presentation of the script. For added enjoyment invite students to think of their own unique motions and movements for the lyrics.

PROPS

No props are needed for this script. If you wish, obtain some plastic ears from a local toy store (frequently available around Halloween time). Invite the students to sing the song while you simulate the various movements with the artificial ears.

DELIVERY

The delivery should be joyous and fun. This is a song that youngsters will be singing again and again, so be sure to keep the emphasis on its light and silly nature.

MUSICAL VERSION

Log on to the following Web site for an easy-to-follow version of this song: http://www.niehs. nih.gov/kids/lyrics/doyourears.htm.

MOVEMENT/DANCE

Instead of a separate movement/dance activity, the movements that students can use for this script are contained within this readers theatre presentation. Invite a select group of characters to present the script to the entire class. Afterward ask the class to do a whole group presentation of the script (the characters can say their lines and the class members can simulate the various movements). Be sure to include the song along with any presentation.

Do Your Ears Hang Low?

STAGING: The characters should all be standing. The scripts should be placed on music stands (thus leaving the characters' hands free to perform the motions indicated in the script). As each character finishes saying her or his line, the other characters perform the motion described in the script. There is no narrator for this script.

Abby	Bobbie	Cathy	David	Erin
X	X	X	X	X

ABBY: Do your ears hang low? [hands on side of head with fingers pointing down]

BOBBIE: Do they wobble to and fro? [wiggle fingers]

CATHY: Can you tie them in a knot? [simulate tying a large knot with hands]

DAVID: Can you tie them in a bow? [simulate tying a large bow with hands]

ERIN: Can you throw them o'er your shoulder like a Continental Soldier? [simulate throwing a large load over the right shoulder]

ALL: Do your ears hang low?

ABBY: Does your tongue hang down? [stick tongue out]

BOBBIE: Does it flop all around? [wiggle tongue]

CATHY: Can you tie it in a knot? [simulate tying a large knot with hands]

DAVID: Can you tie it in a bow? [simulate tying a large bow with hands]

ERIN: Can you throw it o'er your shoulder like a Continental Soldier? [simulate throwing a large load over the right shoulder]

ALL: Does your tongue hang down?

From *Songs and Rhymes Readers Theatre for Beginning Readers* by Anthony D. Fredericks. Westport, CT: Teacher Ideas Press. Copyright © 2008.

ABBY: Does your nose hang low? [bend over at the waist]

BOBBIE: Does it wiggle to and fro? [shake head back and forth]

CATHY: Can you tie it in a knot? [simulate tying a large knot with hands]

DAVID: Can you tie it in a bow? [simulate tying a large bow with hands]

ERIN: Can you throw it o'er your shoulder like a Continental Soldier? [simulate throwing a large load over the right shoulder]

ALL: Does your nose hang low?

ABBY: Do your eyes pop out? [open both eyes wide]

BOBBIE: Do they bounce all about? [shake head back and forth]

CATHY: Can you tie them in a knot? [simulate tying a large knot with hands]

DAVID: Can you tie them in a bow? [simulate tying a large bow with hands]

ERIN: Can you throw them o'er your shoulder like a Continental Soldier? [simulate throwing a large load over the right shoulder]

ALL: Do your eyes pop out?

ABBY: Do your eyeballs droop? [wiggle fingers in front of eyes]

BOBBIE: Do they wobble in your soup? [simulate eating soup with a spoon]

CATHY: Can you tie them in a loop? [simulate tying a large loop with hands]

DAVID: Can you wind them on a hoop? [rotate hand in large circle]

ERIN: Can you throw them o'er your shoulder like a Continental Soldier? [simulate throwing a large load over the right shoulder]

ALL: Do your eyeballs droop?

[Repeat at a somewhat faster clip.]

ABBY: Do your ears hang low? [hands on side of head with fingers pointing down]

BOBBIE: Do they wobble to and fro? [wiggle fingers]

CATHY: Can you tie them in a knot? [simulate tying a large knot with hands]

DAVID: Can you tie them in a bow? [simulate tying a large bow with hands]

ERIN: Can you throw them o'er your shoulder like a Continental Soldier? [simulate throwing a large load over the right shoulder]

ALL: Do your ears hang low?

ABBY: Does your tongue hang down? [stick tongue out]

BOBBIE: Does it flop all around? [wiggle tongue]

CATHY: Can you tie it in a knot? [simulate tying a large knot with hands]

DAVID: Can you tie it in a bow? [simulate tying a large bow with hands]

ERIN: Can you throw it o'er your shoulder like a Continental Soldier? [simulate throwing a large load over the right shoulder]

ALL: Does your tongue hang down?

ABBY: Does your nose hang low? [bend over at the waist]

BOBBIE: Does it wiggle to and fro? [shake head back and forth]

CATHY: Can you tie it in a knot? [simulate tying a large knot with hands]

DAVID: Can you tie it in a bow? [simulate tying a large bow with hands]

ERIN: Can you throw it o'er your shoulder like a Continental Soldier? [simulate throwing a large load over the right shoulder]

ALL: Does your nose hang low?

ABBY: Do your eyes pop out? [open both eyes wide]

BOBBIE: Do they bounce all about? [shake head back and forth]

CATHY: Can you tie them in a knot? [simulate tying a large knot with hands]

DAVID: Can you tie them in a bow? [simulate tying a large bow with hands]

ERIN: Can you throw them o'er your shoulder like a Continental Soldier? [simulate throwing a large load over the right shoulder]

ALL: Do your eyes pop out?

ABBY: Do your eyeballs droop? [wiggle fingers in front of eyes]

BOBBIE: Do they wobble in your soup? [simulate eating soup with a spoon]

CATHY: Can you tie them in a loop? [simulate tying a large loop with hands]

DAVID: Can you wind them on a hoop? [rotate hand in large circle]

ERIN: Can you throw them o'er your shoulder like a Continental Soldier? [simulate throwing a large load over the right shoulder]

ALL: Do your eyeballs droop?

The Wheels on the Bus

PRESENTATION SUGGESTIONS

This script is simply the entire song—there is no additional material. You may wish to introduce the music to students in advance of the presentation. Or you may invite students to put on a single presentation, listen to the music, and then repeat the presentation as the music is playing in the background.

PROPS

No props are necessary for this production. However, you may wish to display a picture of a school bus on the wall behind the presenters.

DELIVERY

The first reading of the script should be at a comfortable rate. After students have become familiar with the words and music, they can be encouraged to "go though" the script at a much faster pace.

MUSICAL VERSION

Log on to the following Web site for an appropriate version of the music: http://www.niehs. nih.gov/kids/lyrics/wheels.htm.

Play the music for students and then invite them to sing the song along with the accompanying music.

MOVEMENT/DANCE

Invite the entire class to participate in this popular song. Ask all the students to stand and engage in the physical activities as the music is playing and the lyrics are being sung.

The wheels on the bus
Go round and round,
[Roll hands over each other.]
Round and round,
[Roll hands over each other.]
Round and round.
[Roll hands over each other.]
The wheels on the bus
Go round and round,
[Roll hands over each other.]
All over town.
[Spread arms open wide.]

The doors on the bus
Swing open and shut,
[Arms in front—open and close.]
Open and shut,
[Arms in front—open and close.]
Open and shut.
[Arms in front—open and close.]
The doors on the bus
Swing open and shut,
[Arms in front—open and close.]
All over town.
[Spread arms open wide.]

The wiper on the bus
Goes swish, swish, swish,
[Hold arms at angle and go back and forth.]
Swish, swish, swish,
[Hold arms at angle and go back and forth.]
Swish, swish, swish.
[Hold arms at angle and go back and forth.]
The wiper on the bus
Goes swish, swish, swish,
[Hold arms at angle and go back and forth.]

All over town.
[Spread arms open wide.]

The horn on the bus
Goes beep, beep, beep,
[Pretend to honk horn.]
Beep, beep, beep,
[Pretend to honk horn.]
Beep, beep, beep.
[Pretend to honk horn.]
The horn on the bus
Goes beep, beep, beep,
[Pretend to honk horn.]
All over town.
[Spread arms open wide.]

The baby on the bus
Goes wah, wah, wah,
[Hands over face pretending to cry.]
Wah, wah, wah,
[Hands over face pretending to cry.]
Wah, wah, wah.
[Hands over face pretending to cry.]
The baby on the bus
Goes wah, wah, wah,
[Hands over face pretending to cry.]
All over town.
[Spread arms open wide.]

The wheels on the bus
Go round and round,
[Roll hands over each other.]
Round and round,
[Roll hands over each other.]
Round and round.
[Roll hands over each other.]
The wheels on the bus
Go round and round,
[Roll hands over each other.]
All over town.
[Spread arms open wide.]

The Wheels on the Bus

STAGING: The characters should all be standing in a loose circle. As the script is being read the students should walk round and round in a slow circle. There is no narrator for this presentation.

```
                              Number 1
                                 X
          Number 6                              Number 2
             X                                     X

          Number 5                              Number 3
             X                                     X
                              Number 4
                                 X
```

NUMBER 1: The wheels on the bus

NUMBER 2: Go round and round,

NUMBER 3: Round and round,

NUMBER 4: Round and round.

NUMBER 5: The wheels on the bus

NUMBER 6: Go round and round,

ALL: All over town.

NUMBER 1: The doors on the bus

NUMBER 2: Swing open and shut,

NUMBER 3: Open and shut,

NUMBER 4: Open and shut.

NUMBER 5: The doors on the bus

NUMBER 6: Swing open and shut,

ALL: All over town.

NUMBER 1: The wiper on the bus

NUMBER 2: Goes swish, swish, swish,

NUMBER 3: Swish, swish, swish,

NUMBER 4: Swish, swish, swish.

NUMBER 5: The wiper on the bus

NUMBER 6: Goes swish, swish, swish,

ALL: All over town.

NUMBER 1: The horn on the bus

NUMBER 2: Goes beep, beep, beep,

NUMBER 3: Beep, beep, beep,

NUMBER 4: Beep, beep, beep.

NUMBER 5: The horn on the bus

NUMBER 6: Goes beep, beep, beep,

ALL: All over town.

NUMBER 1: The baby on the bus

NUMBER 2: Goes wah, wah, wah,

NUMBER 3: Wah, wah, wah,

NUMBER 4: Wah, wah, wah.

NUMBER 5: The baby on the bus

NUMBER 6: Goes wah, wah, wah,

ALL: All over town.

NUMBER 1: The wheels on the bus

NUMBER 2: Go round and round,

NUMBER 3: Round and round,

NUMBER 4: Round and round.

NUMBER 5: The wheels on the bus

NUMBER 6: Go round and round,

ALL: All over town.

[The presenters will repeat the script, but at a much faster pace.]

NUMBER 1:   The wheels on the bus

NUMBER 2:   Go round and round,

NUMBER 3:   Round and round,

NUMBER 4:   Round and round.

NUMBER 5:   The wheels on the bus

NUMBER 6:   Go round and round,

ALL: All over town.

NUMBER 1:   The doors on the bus

NUMBER 2:   Swing open and shut,

NUMBER 3:   Open and shut,

NUMBER 4:   Open and shut.

NUMBER 5:   The doors on the bus

NUMBER 6:   Swing open and shut,

ALL: All over town.

NUMBER 1:   The wiper on the bus

NUMBER 2:   Goes swish, swish, swish,

NUMBER 3:   Swish, swish, swish,

NUMBER 4:   Swish, swish, swish.

NUMBER 5:   The wiper on the bus

NUMBER 6:   Goes swish, swish, swish,

ALL: All over town.

NUMBER 1:   The horn on the bus

NUMBER 2:   Goes beep, beep, beep,

NUMBER 3:   Beep, beep, beep,

NUMBER 4: Beep, beep, beep.

NUMBER 5: The horn on the bus

NUMBER 6: Goes beep, beep, beep,

ALL: All over town.

NUMBER 1: The baby on the bus

NUMBER 2: Goes wah, wah, wah,

NUMBER 3: Wah, wah, wah,

NUMBER 4: Wah, wah, wah.

NUMBER 5: The baby on the bus

NUMBER 6: Goes wah, wah, wah,

ALL: All over town.

NUMBER 1: The wheels on the bus

NUMBER 2: Go round and round,

NUMBER 3: Round and round,

NUMBER 4: Round and round.

NUMBER 5: The wheels on the bus

NUMBER 6: Go round and round,

ALL: All over town.

Resources

READERS THEATRE BOOKS

Barchers, S. *Fifty Fabulous Fables: Beginning Readers Theatre.* Westport, CT: Teacher Ideas Press, 1997.

———. *Judge for Yourself.* Westport, CT: Teacher Ideas Press, 2004.

———. *Multicultural Folktales: Readers Theatre for Elementary Students.* Westport, CT: Teacher Ideas Press, 2000.

———. *Readers Theatre for Beginning Readers.* Westport, CT: Teacher Ideas Press, 1993.

———. *Scary Readers Theatre.* Westport, CT: Teachers Ideas Press, 1994.

Barchers, S., and C. R. Pfeffinger. *Getting Ready to Read with Readers Theatre.* Westport, CT: Teacher Ideas Press, 2007.

———. *More Readers Theatre for Beginning Readers.* Westport, CT: Teacher Ideas Press, 2006.

Barnes, J. W. *Sea Songs.* Westport, CT: Teacher Ideas Press, 2004.

Black, A. N. *Born Storytellers.* Westport, CT: Teacher Ideas Press, 2005.

Criscoe, B. L., and P. J. Lanasa. *Fairy Tales for Two Readers.* Westport, CT: Teacher Ideas Press, 1995.

Dixon, N., A. Davies, and C. Politano. *Learning with Readers Theatre: Building Connections.* Winnipeg, MB: Peguis Publishers, 1996.

Fredericks, A. D. *African Legends, Myths, and Folktales for Readers Theatre.* Westport, CT: Teacher Ideas Press, 2008.

———. *Frantic Frogs and Other Frankly Fractured Folktales for Readers Theatre.* Westport, CT: Teacher Ideas Press, 1993.

———. *MORE Frantic Frogs and Other Frankly Fractured Folktales for Readers Theatre.* Westport, CT: Teacher Ideas Press, 2008.

———. *Mother Goose Readers Theatre for Beginning Readers.* Westport, CT: Teacher Ideas Press, 2007.

———. *Nonfiction Readers Theatre for Beginning Readers.* Westport, CT: Teacher Ideas Press, 2007.

———. *Readers Theatre for American History.* Westport, CT: Teacher Ideas Press, 2001.

———. *Science Fiction Readers Theatre.* Westport, CT: Teacher Ideas Press, 2002.

———. *Silly Salamanders and Other Slightly Stupid Stories for Readers Theatre.* Westport, CT: Teacher Ideas Press, 2000.

———. *Tadpole Tales and Other Totally Terrific Treats for Readers Theatre.* Westport, CT: Teacher Ideas Press, 1997.

Garner, J. *Wings of Fancy: Using Readers Theatre to Study Fantasy Genre.* Westport, CT: Teacher Ideas Press, 2006

Georges, C., and C. Cornett. *Reader's Theatre*. Buffalo, NY: D.O.K. Publishers, 1990.

Haven, K. *Great Moments in Science: Experiments and Readers Theatre*. Westport, CT: Teacher Ideas Press, 1996.

Jenkins, D. R. *Just Deal with It*. Westport, CT: Teacher Ideas Press, 2004.

Johnson, T. D., and D. R. Louis. *Bringing It All Together: A Program for Literacy*. Portsmouth, NH: Heinemann, 1990.

Latrobe, K. H., C. Casey, and L. A. Gann. *Social Studies Readers Theatre for Young Adults*. Westport, CT: Teacher Ideas Press, 1991.

Laughlin, M. K., P. T. Black, and K. H. Latrobe. *Social Studies Readers Theatre for Children*. Westport, CT: Teacher Ideas Press, 1991.

Laughlin, M. K., and K. H. Latrobe. *Readers Theatre for Children*. Westport, CT: Teacher Ideas Press, 1990.

Martin, J. M. *12 Fabulously Funny Fairy Tale Plays*. New York: Instructor Books, 2002.

Peterson, C. *Around the World Through Holidays*. Westport, CT: Teacher Ideas Press, 2005.

Pfeffinger, C. R. *Character Counts*. Westport, CT: Teacher Ideas Press, 2003.

———. *Holiday Readers Theatre*. Westport, CT: Teacher Ideas Press, 1994.

Pugliano-Martin, C. *25 Just-Right Plays for Emergent Readers (Grades K–1)*. New York: Scholastic, 1999.

Shepard, A. *Folktales on Stage: Children's Plays for Readers Theatre*. Olympia, WA: Shepard Publications, 2003.

———. *Readers on Stage: Resources for Readers Theatre*. Olympia, WA: Shepard Publications, 2004.

———. *Stories on Stage: Children's Plays for Readers Theatre*. Olympia, WA: Shepard Publications, 2005.

Sloyer, S. *From the Page to the Stage*. Westport, CT: Teacher Ideas Press, 2003.

Wolf, J. M. *Cinderella Outgrows the Glass Slipper and Other Zany Fractured Fairy Tale Plays*. New York: Scholastic, 2002.

Wolfman, J. *How and Why Stories for Readers Theatre*. Westport, CT: Teacher Ideas Press, 2004.

Worthy, J. *Readers Theatre for Building Fluency: Strategies and Scripts for Making the Most of This Highly Effective, Motivating, and Research-Based Approach to Oral Reading*. New York: Scholastic, 2005.

WEB SITES

http://www.aaronshep.com/rt/RTE.html

How to use readers theatre, sample scripts from a children's author who specializes in readers theatre, and an extensive list of resources.

http://www.cdli.ca/CITE/langrt.htm

This site has lots of information, including "What Is Readers Theatre," "Readers Theatre Scripts," "Writing Scripts," "Recommended Print Resources," and "Recommended On-line Resources."

http://www.teachingheart.net/readerstheater.htm
> Here you discover lots of plays and scripts to print and read in your classroom or library.

http://literacyconnections.com/readerstheater
> There is an incredible number of resources and scripts at this all-inclusive site.

http://www.proteacher.com/070173.shmtl
> This site is a growing collection of tens of thousands of ideas shared by teachers across the United States and around the world.

http://www.readerstheatredigest.com
> This is an online magazine of ideas, scripts, and teaching strategies.

http://www.readerstheatre.escd.net
> This site has more than 150 short poems, stories, and chants for readers theatre.

http://www.storycart.com
> Storycart's Press's subscription service provides an inexpensive opportunity to have timely scripts delivered to teachers or librarians each month. Each script is created or adapted by well-known writer Suzanne Barchers, author of several readers theatre books (see above).

PROFESSIONAL ORGANIZATION

Institute for Readers Theatre
P.O. Box 421262
San Diego, CA 92142
(858) 277-4274
http://www.readerstheatreinstitute.com

More Teacher Resources

by
Anthony D. Fredericks

The following books are available from Teacher Ideas Press (88 Post Road West, Westport, CT 06881); 1-800-225-5800; http://www.teacherideaspress.com.

African Legends, Myths, and Folktales for Readers Theatre. ISBN 1-59158-633-X. ($25.00).
> From the various regions of the African continent comes this engaging and compelling collection of folktales, legends, and stories. "The Lion, the Hare, and the Hyena" (Kenya), "The Roof of Leaves" (Congo), "The Mantis and the Moon" (South Africa), and "Anansi's Fishing Expedition (Ghana), and other tales will introduce youngsters to the rich literary heritage of more than 25 countries.

Frantic Frogs and Other Frankly Fractured Folktales for Readers Theatre. ISBN 1-56308-174-1. (123pp.; $19.50).
> Have you heard "Don't Kiss Sleeping Beauty, She's Got Really Bad Breath" or "The Brussels Sprouts Man (The Gingerbread Man's Unbelievably Strange Cousin)"? This resource (grades 4–8) offers 30 reproducible satirical scripts for rip-roaring dramatics in any classroom or library.

The Integrated Curriculum: Books for Reluctant Readers, Grades 2–5. 2nd ed. ISBN 0-87287-994-1. (220pp.; $22.50).
> This book presents guidelines for motivating and using literature with reluctant readers. The book contains more than 40 book units on titles carefully selected to motivate the most reluctant readers.

Investigating Natural Disasters Through Children's Literature: An Integrated Approach. ISBN 1-56308-861-4. (193pp.; $28.00).
> Tap into students' inherent awe of storms, volcanic eruptions, hurricanes, earthquakes, tornadoes, floods, avalanches, landslides, and tsunamis to open their minds to the wonders and power of the natural world.

Involving Parents Through Children's Literature: P–K. ISBN 1-56308-022-2. (86pp.; $15.00).

Involving Parents Through Children's Literature: Grades 1–2. ISBN 1-56308-012-5. (95pp.; $14.50).

Involving Parents Through Children's Literature: Grades 3–4. ISBN 1-56308-013-3. (96pp.; $15.50).

Involving Parents Through Children's Literature: Grades 5–6. ISBN 1-56308-014-1. (107pp.; $16.00).
> This series of books offers engaging activities for adults and children that stimulate comprehension and promote reading enjoyment. Reproducible activity sheets based on high-quality children's books are designed in a convenient format so that children can take them home.

The Librarian's Complete Guide to Involving Parents Through Children's Literature: Grades K–6. ISBN 1-56308-538-0. (137pp.; $24.50).

Activities for 101 children's books are presented in a reproducible format, so librarians can distribute them to students to take home and share with parents.

MORE Social Studies Through Children's Literature: An Integrated Approach. ISBN 1-56308-761-8. (225pp.; $27.50).

Energize your social studies curriculum with dynamic, "hands-on, minds-on" projects based on such great children's books as *Amazing Grace*, *Fly Away Home*, and *Lon Po Po*. This book is filled with an array of activities and projects sure to "energize" any social studies curriculum.

Mother Goose Readers Theatre for Beginning Readers. ISBN 1-59158-500-7. (188pp.; $25.00).

Written for children reading at first- and second-grade levels, this readers theatre book uses Mother Goose rhymes as its basis, making it especially valuable to teachers and librarians working on building fluency skills in their beginning readers. The book offers plays based on well-known rhymes, complete with presentation and instructional follow-up suggestions. Several of the scripts feature simultaneous Spanish translations—a real plus for ELL programs.

Much MORE Social Studies Through Children's Literature: A Collaborative Approach. ISBN 1-59158-445-0. (276pp.; $35.00).

These dynamic, literature-based activities will help teachers and librarians energize the entire social studies curriculum and implement national (and state) standards. This book presents hundreds of "hands-on, minds-on" projects that actively engage students in positive learning experiences. Each of the 62 units offers book summaries, social studies topic areas, critical thinking questions, classroom resources, and lots of easy-to-do activities for every grade level.

Nonfiction Readers Theatre for Beginning Readers. ISBN 1-59158-499-X. (220pp.; $25.00).

Teachers are continually looking for an interesting, fun way to input content knowledge to build that background information that will help push up expository reading scores. This book offers 30 short nonfiction readers theatre plays for the young reader (grades 1–3) on topics ranging from earth and natural sciences to community helpers, holidays, and government. All topics are tied to curriculum common in the primary grades.

Readers Theatre for American History. ISBN 1-56308-860-6. (173pp.; $30.00).

This book offers a participatory approach to American history in which students become active participants in several historical events. These 24 scripts give students a "you are there" perspective on critical milestones and colorful moments that have shaped the American experience.

Science Adventures with Children's Literature: A Thematic Approach. ISBN 1-56308-417-1. (190pp.; $24.50).

Focusing on the National Science Education Standards, this activity-centered resource uses a wide variety of children's literature to integrate science across the elementary curriculum. With a thematic approach, it features the best in science trade books along with stimulating "hands-on, minds-on" activities in all the sciences.

Science Discoveries on the Net: An Integrated Approach. ISBN 1-56308-823-1. (315pp.; $27.50).

This book is designed to help teachers integrate the Internet into their science programs and enhance the scientific discoveries of students. The 88 units emphasize key concepts—based on national and state standards—throughout the science curriculum.

Silly Salamanders and Other Slightly Stupid Stuff for Readers Theatre. ISBN 1-56308-825-8. (161pp.; $23.50).

The third entry in the "wild and wacky" readers theatre trilogy is just as crazy and just as weird as the first two. This unbelievable resource offers students in grades 3–6 dozens of silly send-ups of well-known fairy tales, legends, and original stories.

Social Studies Discoveries on the Net: An Integrated Approach. ISBN 1-56308-824-X. (276pp.; $26.00).

This book is designed to help teachers integrate the Internet into their social studies programs and enhance the classroom discoveries of students. The 75 units emphasize key concepts—based on national and state standards—throughout the social studies curriculum.

Social Studies Through Children's Literature: An Integrated Approach. ISBN 1-87287-970-4. (192pp.; $24.00),

Each of the 32 instructional units contained in this resource utilizes an activity-centered approach to elementary social studies, featuring children's picture books such as *Ox-Cart Man, In Coal Country,* and *Jambo Means Hello.*

Tadpole Tales and Other Totally Terrific Titles for Readers Theatre. ISBN 1-56308-547-X. (115pp.; $18.50).

A follow-up volume to the best-selling *Frantic Frogs and Other Frankly Fractured Folktales for Readers Theatre,* this book provides primary-level readers (grades 1–4) with a humorous assortment of wacky tales based on well-known Mother Goose rhymes. More than 30 scripts and dozens of extensions will keep students rolling in the aisles.

Index

About the Author

Anthony (Tony) D. Fredericks (afredericks60@comcast.net) is a nationally recognized children's literature expert well known for his energetic, humorous, and highly informative school visits throughout North America. His dynamic author presentations have captivated thousands of students in Canada, Mexico, and across the United States—all with rave reviews!

Tony is a former elementary teacher and reading specialist. He is the author of more than 100 books, including more than 65 teacher resource books and more than three-dozen award-winning children's books. His education titles include the best-selling *The Complete Phonemic Awareness Handbook* (Harcourt Achieve), the hugely popular *Nonfiction Readers Theatre for Beginning Readers* (Teacher Ideas Press), the highly praised *Guided Reading in Grades K–2* (Harcourt Achieve), and the celebrated *Much More Social Studies Through Children's Literature* (Teacher Ideas Press).

His award-winning children's titles include *Under One Rock* (2002 Nature and Ecology Award), *Slugs* (2000 Outstanding Science Trade Book), *Around One Cactus* (2004 Teacher's Choice Award), *Near One Cattail* (2006 Green Earth Book Award), and *The Tsunami Quilt: Grandfather's Story,* among others.

Fredericks is the author of several trade books, including the acclaimed *The Complete Idiot's Guide to Teaching College* (Alpha). Tony currently teaches elementary methods courses and children's literature at York College in York, Pennsylvania.

RECENT TITLES IN TEACHER IDEAS PRESS' READERS THEATRE SERIES

Simply Shakespeare: Readers Theatre for Young People
Edited by Jennifer L. Kroll

Character Counts! Promoting Character Education Through Readers Theatre, Grades 2–5
Charla Rene Pfeffinger

Sea Songs: Readers Theatre from the South Pacific
James W. Barnes

Judge for Yourself: Famous American Trials for Readers Theatre
Suzanne I. Barchers

Just Deal with It! Funny Readers Theatre for Life's Not-So-Funny Moments
Diana R. Jenkins

How and Why Stories for Readers Theatre
Judy Wolfman

Born Storytellers: Readers Theatre Celebrates the Lives and Literature of Classic Authors
Ann N. Black

Around the World Through Holidays: Cross Curricular Readers Theatre
Written and Illustrated by Carol Peterson

Wings of Fancy: Using Readers Theatre to Study Fantasy Genre
Joan Garner

Nonfiction Readers Theatre for Beginning Readers
Anthony D. Fredericks

Mother Goose Readers Theatre for Beginning Readers
Anthony D. Fredericks

MORE Frantic Frogs and Other Frankly Fractured Folktales for Readers Theatre
Anthony D. Fredericks